MASTER INTRADAY TRADING WITH CPR & PIVOTS

POWERFUL AND EFFECTIVE INTRADAY TRADING STRATEGIES FOR CONSISTENT EARNING

ANWESHA PANDA

Copyright © Anwesha Panda
All Rights Reserved.

This book has been self-published with all reasonable efforts taken to make the material error-free by the author. No part of this book shall be used, reproduced in any manner whatsoever without written permission from the author, except in the case of brief quotations embodied in critical articles and reviews.

The Author of this book is solely responsible and liable for its content including but not limited to the views, representations, descriptions, statements, information, opinions and references ["Content"]. The Content of this book shall not constitute or be construed or deemed to reflect the opinion or expression of the Publisher or Editor. Neither the Publisher nor Editor endorse or approve the Content of this book or guarantee the reliability, accuracy or completeness of the Content published herein and do not make any representations or warranties of any kind, express or implied, including but not limited to the implied warranties of merchantability, fitness for a particular purpose. The Publisher and Editor shall not be liable whatsoever for any errors, omissions, whether such errors or omissions result from negligence, accident, or any other cause or claims for loss or damages of any kind, including without limitation, indirect or consequential loss or damage arising out of use, inability to use, or about the reliability, accuracy or sufficiency of the information contained in this book.

Made with ♥ on the Notion Press Platform
www.notionpress.com

I dedicate this book to my father, Bibhas Chandra Panda, whose encouragement led me to venture into the Indian Stock Market. His boundless guidance and wisdom have been my compass through this journey. Can we ever thank a father enough? Not sure.

My dearest husband, Pratyut, who has been a constant source of strength and support. His unwavering love and encouragement have pushed me forward and reminded me of my potential and worth. He is my confidant and my biggest cheerleader. His belief in me is my greatest motivation, and his understanding and love have created a nurturing environment where I can pursue my passions wholeheartedly. I am truly blessed to have him as my life partner. This book is as much his as it is mine, as it reflects the shared dreams, joys, and challenges we have faced together.

My grandfather, late Dr. Nrusingh Charan Panda, whose legacy of knowledge and dedication continues to inspire me.

Contents

Contents

Preface

Let me admit that I am not a student of finance. Being a student of Electrical Engineering, I found it quite difficult to understand the details and complexities of financial markets. Certainly, trading is not as easy a profession as most people think. The learning curve is so steep that beginners often incur huge losses and eventually exit the stock markets. One needs to have a strong drive, dedication, and fascination for financial markets to emerge as a successful trader. Intraday trading, often considered the most difficult form of trading, comes with enormous risks and stress. My main motive for writing this book is to create a shortcut for new traders; it contains the kind of information I wish I could have received when I was getting started. Even though there are no shortcuts to success or holy grail strategies in stock markets, I hope this book will help you develop an edge in trading. I have tried my level best to write this book in simple language so that beginners can grasp all the concepts easily and trade with minimal risk and maximum confidence.

I have used all the charts and trading tools from the website Tradingview.com

I hope you will enjoy reading this book to the fullest!

Acknowledgements

I would like to extend my deep gratitude and sincere thanks to all my fellow traders, investors and mentors who have played a part, big or small, in shaping my journey as a trader. They have handheld me through the tricky terrain and answered my naive questions with enormous patience and indulgence.

Disclaimer

This book is meant to be informational and for educational purposes. It is meant to help readers improve their trading skills. If anyone, after reading this book, does trading or invests in financial markets and under any circumstances, due to any reason incurs losses, then the author, publisher and/or seller are not responsible for the losses. One should trade responsibly with adequate knowledge of the financial markets and with proper risk management.

About The Author

Anwesha Panda is a graduate in Electrical Engineering. After a brief stint in the corporate world, she quit her job to turn into a full-time trader. When she is not busy dabbling in the stock markets, she loves to spill her creativity by writing and painting. You can reach out to her at ap.workspace97@gmail.com or tweet her @aanwessha.

CHAPTER I

INTRODUCTION TO CENTRAL PIVOT RANGE (CPR) & PIVOT POINTS

CENTRAL PIVOT RANGE (CPR)

The Central Pivot Range (CPR) is a technical analysis indicator used by traders in financial markets such as stocks, futures, and commodities. Its primary purpose is to identify potential support and resistance levels for a given time period and to forecast the trend of a particular financial instrument. CPR finds application in intraday trading, swing trading, as well as positional trading strategies. It utilizes the previous trading day's high, low, and close prices to calculate key support and resistance levels for the current trading day. In essence, CPR consists of three lines representing these key levels, collectively known as the Central Pivot Range. Traders integrate these levels with other technical analysis tools to inform their trading decisions, including the determination of entry and exit points for trades.

KEY LEVELS OF CENTRAL PIVOT RANGE (CPR)

The three key levels of Central Pivot Range (CPR) are:

1. **Central Pivot Point:** The Central Pivot Point (CPP) serves as the midpoint between the previous day's high,

low, and close prices. It is calculated using the formula: CPP = (Previous High + Previous Low + Previous Close) / 3.

2. **Top CPR (TCPR):** The Top CPR is derived by adding the difference between the previous day's high and low to the Central Pivot Point. Mathematically, TCPR = Central Pivot Point + (Previous High - Previous Low).

3. **Bottom CPR (BCPR):** Conversely, the Bottom CPR is obtained by subtracting the difference between the previous day's high and low from the Central Pivot Point. The formula for BCPR is BCPR = Central Pivot Point - (Previous High - Previous Low).

Understanding and utilizing these key levels of the CPR can assist traders in identifying potential price reversal points, determining entry and exit levels for trades, and effectively managing risk within their trading strategies.

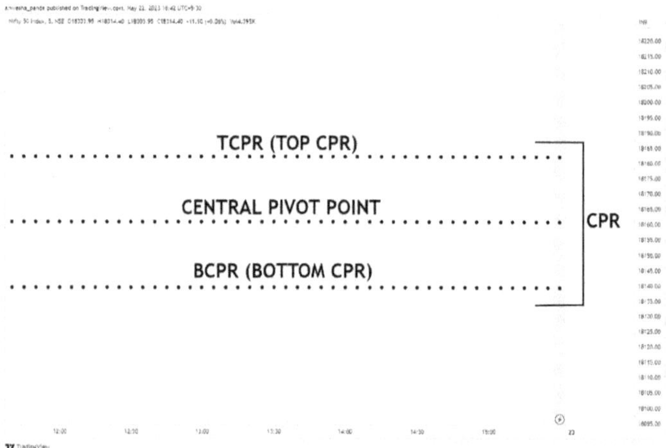

Figure (1.1)

Figure (1.1) illustrates the Central Pivot Range (CPR). The line above the central pivot point is termed as the Top CPR (TCPR), while the line below the central pivot point is referred to as the Bottom CPR (BCPR). The Central Pivot Range (CPR) encompasses this entire range or combination of these three lines.

PIVOT POINTS

Pivot points are support and resistance lines calculated based on the average prices of the high, low, and close of the previous day, week, and month. Traders use these lines to identify potential price levels where the market may reverse, encounter resistance, or find support.

The combination of CPR and pivot points provides traders with a comprehensive framework for trading. While these indicators may appear complex on charts, they essentially represent straightforward support and resistance lines. Technical analysts use CPR to gauge the overall market sentiment and identify potential trading prospects. CPR indicates where the market is likely to face support and resistance and can also be used to identify potential price reversals, breakout opportunities, and to set profit targets and stop-loss levels. Additionally, CPR helps traders gauge the overall market sentiment and make informed trading decisions based on the price action around these key levels.

Unlike other indicators such as MACD or RSI, CPR serves as a leading indicator. Pivot points and CPR remain static on the chart and do not change their values or positions with any alterations in the time frame. Their values and positions remain constant across various chart intervals, including 1-minute, 5-minute, 15-minute, 1-hour, and 1-day charts. Once plotted, their location on the chart remains unchanged from the market's opening to its closing. Being a leading indicator, CPR provides signals well in advance compared to lagging indicators, which offer delayed signals. Early signals can assist traders in determining potential trades, understanding market trends, and gauging other market sentiments well in advance.

Refer to the image below to see how pivot lines appear on the chart.

```
___________________________________ R4
___________________________________ R3
___________________________________ R2
___________________________________ R1
___________________________________ S1
___________________________________ S2
___________________________________ S3
___________________________________ S4
```

R1, R2, R3, R4, S1, S2, S3, and S4 are pivot points or pivot lines. R1, R2, R3, R4 denote resistance lines, while S1, S2, S3, S4 represent support lines. In simple terms, these lines or levels on a chart indicate where the price of a particular trading instrument is likely to encounter support or resistance. Resistance lines are typically marked in red, and support lines are marked in green, enhancing clarity on the chart. This color differentiation makes it easier to identify these levels and make informed trading decisions based on candlestick formations near these lines.

Figure (1.2) depicts CPR and pivot lines plotted on a 5-minute timeframe chart representing the Nifty 50 Index.

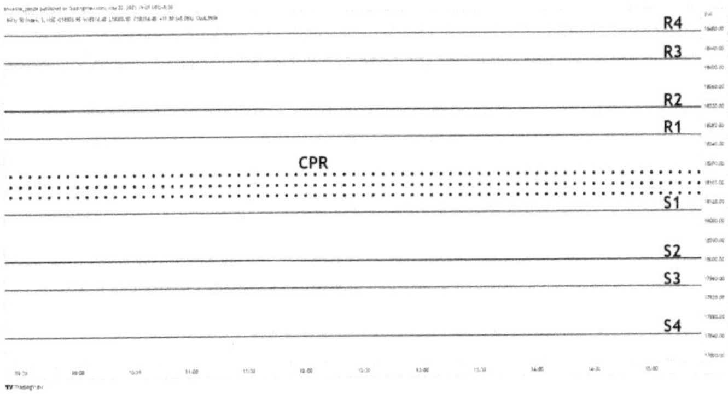

Figure (1.2)

Traders can rely on these pivot point lines to anticipate potential areas where prices of various financial instruments might encounter significant buying or selling pressure. For instance, when a price of any financial instrument approaches a resistance level such as R1, R2, R3, or R4, traders often interpret this as a signal to consider selling positions or taking profits on existing trades. On the other hand, approaching support levels like S1, S2, S3, or S4 may trigger buying activity or decisions to hold existing positions for support.

These pivot point levels can be manually plotted on charts using calculations based on the previous day's high, low, and close prices. Alternatively, traders can access these levels conveniently through various charting softwares and trading platforms, streamlining their analysis process.

What makes pivot points particularly versatile is their ability to identify key support and resistance levels dynamically, reflecting changes in market sentiment and price action on a daily basis. This flexibility makes them valuable for traders across different timeframes, including intraday, swing, and positional trading strategies.

By integrating pivot points with other technical analysis tools, traders can gain deeper insights into potential entry and exit points. Additionally, the collective analysis helps traders in forecasting market trends more effectively, enhancing their overall trading strategies and decision-making processes.

• • •

CHAPTER II

ADVANTAGES OF CPR & PIVOT POINTS IN TECHNICAL ANALYSIS

With numerous indicators available today, what sets the CPR indicator apart for intraday trading compared to others in platforms like TradingView and other charting softwares? I'd like to delve into these questions further with the help of a few charts.

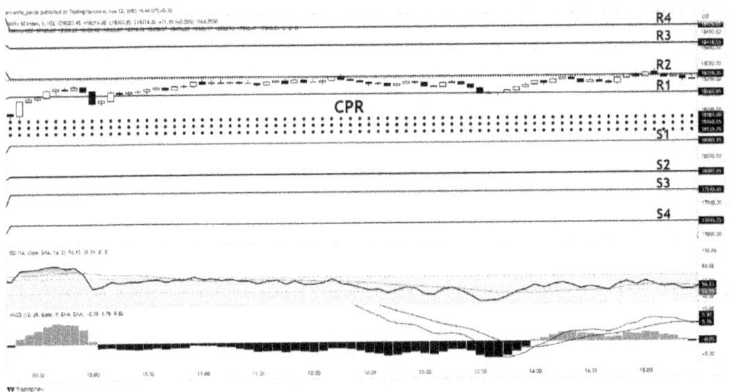

Figure (2.1)

Figure (2.1) depicts CPR, pivot lines, MACD, and RSI plotted on a 5-minute chart of the Nifty 50 Index on May 22, 2023. The chart distinctly illustrates that CPR and pivot lines remain unchanged throughout the trading session. They maintained consistent values and positions from market open to market close, in contrast to lagging indicators such as RSI and MACD, which fluctuated multiple times in response to price changes during the trading hours.

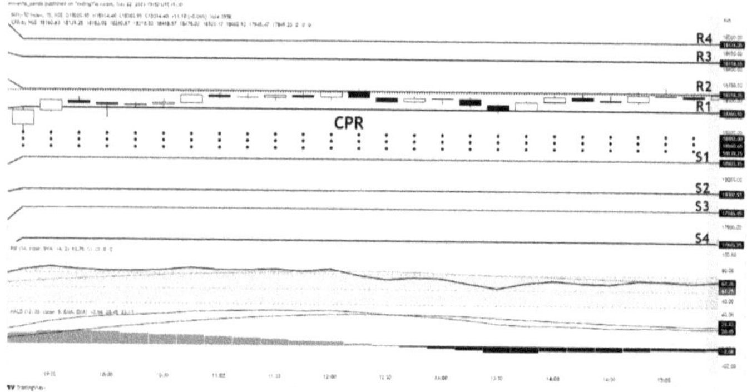

Figure (2.2)

Figure (2.2) illustrates indicators such as CPR, pivot lines, MACD, and RSI plotted on a 15-minute chart of the Nifty 50 Index on May 22, 2023. The chart clearly demonstrates that CPR and pivot lines remain unchanged even on the 15-minute chart. They maintain a consistent position and value regardless of changes in the timeframe. In contrast, RSI and MACD exhibit variations in their values and positions when transitioning from a 5-minute to a 15-minute timeframe. This observation highlights that lagging indicators like RSI, MACD, and others alter their signals with changes in timeframe, potentially confusing traders and making profitable trading decisions more challenging. Conversely, CPR and pivot points remain static across different timeframes, offering traders a clear and consistent reference point without the ambiguity and uncertainty associated with lagging indicators. This stability can provide traders with a valuable edge in making profitable trading decisions. Leading indicators like CPR and pivot lines exhibit remarkable consistency, maintaining unchanged values and positions regardless of the timeframe. This stability contrasts sharply with lagging indicators like RSI and MACD, which demonstrate fluctuations in both values and positions as the timeframe shifts. Adding other lagging indicators further accentuates this difference, showcasing how their signals vary across different time intervals. Such comparisons underscore the complexity traders face in interpreting market signals, especially when relying on lagging indicators. The static nature of CPR and pivot points across timeframes offers traders a reliable reference point amidst changing market conditions, potentially aiding in more informed and confident trading decisions.

Comparing Figure (2.1) and Figure (2.2) reveals identical charts displayed in different timeframes. These charts include indicators such as CPR, pivot lines, MACD, and RSI, allowing for a comprehensive analysis of market dynamics across varying time intervals. The observation highlights a notable difference in the behavior of these indicators across various timeframes.

In addition to being a leading indicator that provides advance signals, CPR offers several other advantages.

- CPR is relatively simple to understand and calculate as compared to other complex indicators. It is derived from the basic pivot point calculation and provides traders with a visual representation of support and resistance levels.
- CPR reflects market sentiments. It takes into account the previous day's price action and helps traders gauge the market sentiment for the current trading session. By

analyzing how price movements interact with the CPR range, traders can gain insights into whether the market is bullish, bearish, or range-bound, which can improve their trading decisions.

- CPR acts as an effective intraday trading tool. When CPR is particulary used for intraday trading, it provides short-term support and resistance levels. Traders can use these levels to identify potential price reversals, breakout points, or areas of consolidation, enabling them to plan their trades accordingly.
- CPR has better compatibility with other indicators. CPR can be combined with other technical indicators, such as moving averages, oscillators, supertrend, etc. to enhance the accuracy of trading signals. By using CPR in conjunction with other tools, traders can validate potential trade setups and increase the probability of successful trades.
- CPR can be applied to various financial markets, including stocks, commodities, and indices. Its versatility allows traders to use a consistent indicator across different markets, streamlining their analysis process.
- CPR is very useful for multiple timeframe analysis. CPR can be applied to various timeframes, from intraday to long-term charts. This flexibility enables traders to assess market conditions and potential price levels across different time horizons, facilitating a comprehensive analysis of price action.

While CPR has its advantages, it's crucial to note that no single indicator can guarantee trading success. Traders should always adopt a holistic approach, combining multiple factors such as technical analysis, risk management techniques, and market knowledge to make well-informed trading decisions.

• • •

CHAPTER III

CALCULATION FORMULAS FOR CPR & PIVOT POINTS

The most commonly used method for calculating pivot lines is the standard method, which involves the following calculations.

FORMULA TO CALCULATE CENTRAL PIVOT RANGE (CPR)

- TCPR (Top CPR) = Central Pivot + (High - Low)/4
- Central Pivot = (High + Low + Close)/3
- BCPR (Bottom CPR) = Central Pivot - (High- Low)/4

FORMULA TO CALCULATE PIVOT POINTS

- R1 = (2 x Central Pivot) – Low
- R2 = Central Pivot + (High – Low)
- S1 = (2 x Central Pivot) – High
- S2 = Central Pivot – (High – Low)
- R3 = Central Pivot + 2 x (High – Low)
- S3 = Central Pivot - 2 x (High - Low)
- R4 = Central Pivot + 3 x (High - Low)
- S4 = Central Pivot - 3 x (High - Low)

These formulas use the "High" and "Low" values, representing the highest and lowest prices from the previous period, typically the previous day. They are extensions of the basic support and resistance levels calculated around the Central Pivot.

The additional support levels, S1, S2, S3, and S4, offer traders additional potential price levels that may act as support during downward price movements. Similarly, the additional resistance levels R1, R2, R3, and R4, provide potential price levels that may act as resistance during upward price movements.

These formulas are typically used in financial analysis tools or spreadsheets to calculate pivot points and CPR using a given set of high, low, and close prices. However, the CPR indicator is now available in many charting softwares. Traders can directly add the indicator to the chart without needing to calculate and plot it manually.

● ● ●

CHAPTER IV

IMPORTANT PIVOT POINTS IN INTRADAY TRADING

Daily, weekly, monthly, and yearly pivots serve as fundamental tools in trading, providing critical insights into market dynamics and potential price levels. Among these, daily pivots hold particular significance in intraday trading due to their strength as support and resistance levels on charts. These pivot levels are derived from the previous day's price action and are recalculated at the beginning of each trading session, making them highly relevant for intraday traders.

In intraday trading, the hierarchy of pivot importance typically follows a specific order:

DAILY PIVOTS > WEEKLY PIVOTS > MONTHLY PIVOTS > YEARLY PIVOTS

Daily pivots take precedence due to their proximity to current price action, making them more influential in guiding intraday trading decisions. Traders often prioritize daily pivots as they provide real-time reference points for assessing market sentiment and identifying potential price reversals or breakout opportunities.

For example, suppose a trader is analyzing a 5-minute chart of a stock. Intraday traders would pay close attention to the daily pivot levels, as these levels can act as significant support or resistance zones throughout the trading day. If the price approaches a daily pivot level and shows signs of reversal, traders may consider entering a trade based on the expectation of a price bounce from that level.

In addition to daily pivots, traders may also incorporate weekly and monthly pivots into their analysis for multi-time frame analysis and swing trading strategies. Weekly and monthly pivots provide broader context and can help traders identify long-term support and resistance levels, complementing their intraday trading decisions.

Overall, daily pivots play a crucial role in intraday trading, providing traders with valuable reference points for navigating the market and making informed trading decisions. By understanding the significance of daily pivots and incorporating them into their trading strategies, intraday traders can enhance their ability to capitalize on short-term price movements and achieve consistent profitability.

• • •

CHAPTER V

IDENTIFYING BULLISH & BEARISH TREND USING CPR

The CPR indicator can be instrumental in forecasting market trends, analyzing market direction, predicting potential movements for the upcoming day, and offering much more insight. Furthermore, the placement of CPR can provide a bias about the present or upcoming day, significantly enhancing your trading edge. In trading, having an edge is crucial for profitability, and leveraging tools like CPR can help traders make informed decisions and increase their chances of success.

One of the key advantages of using the CPR indicator is its ability to provide actionable insights into market biases. The placement of CPR levels relative to the current price action can give traders a clear bias for the present day or the upcoming day. Having this bias information can significantly improve a trader's edge in the market. It helps traders make more informed decisions regarding entry and exit points, risk management strategies, and overall trade setups. By combining CPR analysis with other technical indicators or trading strategies, traders can further refine their trading approach and increase their profitability over time.

In essence, the CPR indicator serves as a valuable tool for traders across different timeframes, from intraday to swing trading. It provides a structured framework for understanding market sentiment and price action dynamics, empowering traders to navigate complex market conditions with confidence and precision.

BULLISH TREND

If the price is consistently trading above the CPR levels, it indicates a bullish bias, suggesting potential long opportunities or a strengthening bullish trend.

Figure (5.1)

In Figure (5.1), a 5-minute chart of the Nifty 50 Index on May 4, 2023, is depicted. From the observed price action, it is evident that the formation of candles above the CPR indicates a bullish day. When price action consistently remains above the CPR levels, it signifies strong buying interest and upward momentum in the market. Traders can interpret this as a signal for potential long positions or as confirmation of an ongoing uptrend.

Figure (5.2)

In Figure (5.2), a 5-minute chart of the Nifty Bank Index on March 23, 2023, is depicted. From the observed price action, it is evident that the formation of candles above the CPR indicates a bullish day.

The location of key support and resistance levels within the CPR framework can offer additional confirmation of bullish or bearish sentiment. If the price successfully holds above the CPR levels, it reinforces the bullish outlook. Conversely, a sustained drop below CPR support levels may indicate a shift towards bearish sentiment.

BEARISH TREND

If the price is consistently trading below the CPR levels, it may signal a bearish bias, indicating potential short opportunities or a strengthening bearish trend.

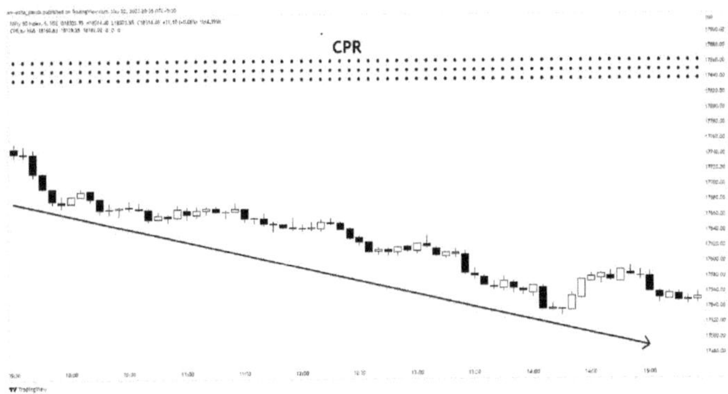

Figure (5.3)

In Figure (5.3), a 5-minute chart of the Nifty 50 Index on February 22, 2023, is depicted. From the observed price action, it is evident that the formation of candles below the CPR indicates a bearish day. This pattern indicates a bearish bias for the trading day, suggesting a dominance of selling pressure and a potential downtrend. When price action consistently remains below the CPR levels, it reflects weak buying interest and potential downward momentum in the market. Traders can interpret this as a signal for potential short positions or as confirmation of an ongoing downtrend.

Figure (5.4)

In Figure (5.4), a 5-minute chart of the Nifty Bank Index on February 22, 2023, is depicted. From the observed price action, it is evident that the formation of candles below the CPR indicates a bearish day. Additionally, analyzing the interactions between price movements and CPR support and resistance levels provides further insights. If the price struggles to rise above CPR support-turned-resistance levels after a downtrend, it reinforces the bearish outlook.

In conclusion, CPR analysis on intraday charts like the 5-minute chart of the Nifty 50 and Nifty Bank Index provides valuable insights into short-term market dynamics. Understanding the interplay between price candles and CPR levels equips traders with a strategic advantage in identifying and capitalizing on bearish or bullish market conditions, thereby enhancing trading profitability and risk management strategies.

• • •

CHAPTER VI

TYPES OF CPR

In this chapter, we will delve into different types of CPR formations and explore their impact on market dynamics through the use of charts and examples. We'll examine how these formations influence price action, and discuss their significance in technical analysis.

WIDE CPR

A wide CPR serves as robust support and resistance lines on a chart, providing valuable insights into market dynamics. When the CPR range is wide, it becomes challenging for candles to breach these levels. Consequently, as the price of a trading instrument nears a wide CPR, candles often find support or resistance at these levels and rebound. This phenomenon makes wide CPR a useful tool for identifying potential price reversals in various trading instruments. Moreover, the width of the CPR also indicates the likelihood of the market remaining range-bound or sideways during a particular trading session. A wide CPR suggests a higher probability of a range-bound market, indicating a potential area of consolidation. In such scenarios, traders should focus on identifying trading opportunities within the established range. This involves taking positions near the upper or lower CPR levels and anticipating price reversals within the range.

For example, consider a scenario where a financial instrument's price approaches a wide CPR range. Traders observing this setup can anticipate that the price will likely struggle to break through the upper or lower boundaries of the CPR range. As a result, when the price nears the CPR level in an uptrend, traders may expect a potential resistance level where the price could reverse or experience a pullback. Similarly, in a downtrend, approaching the CPR level may act as a strong support zone where traders may look for buying opportunities or expect a bounce.

In conclusion, when the CPR range is wide, it indicates a significant price range within which the market is likely to oscillate. Traders can leverage this information to make informed trading decisions and adjust their trading strategies to focus more on range trading techniques.

Figure (6.1)

In Figure (6.1), we observe a 5-minute time-frame chart of the Nifty 50 Index on June 21, 2023. The chart vividly illustrates how a wide Central Pivot Range (CPR) contributes to a range-bound or sideways trading session. This example underscores the significance of analyzing the width of the CPR in forecasting the trend of the day.

Further insights and detailed explanations about this concept will be covered in upcoming chapters.

Figure (6.2)

In Figure (6.2), we can observe a 5-minute chart of the Nifty 50 Index on May 11, 2023. The chart vividly demonstrates how a wide Central Pivot Range (CPR) serves as a strong support level. Each time the candles touch the wide CPR, they receive support, leading to a noticeable bounce-back in price action. This phenomenon not only reinforces the strength of the wide CPR as a support level but also indicates an upward momentum in the price action. Observing such interactions between price movements and CPR levels provides valuable insights for traders, helping them make informed decisions regarding potential price reversals and overall market sentiment.

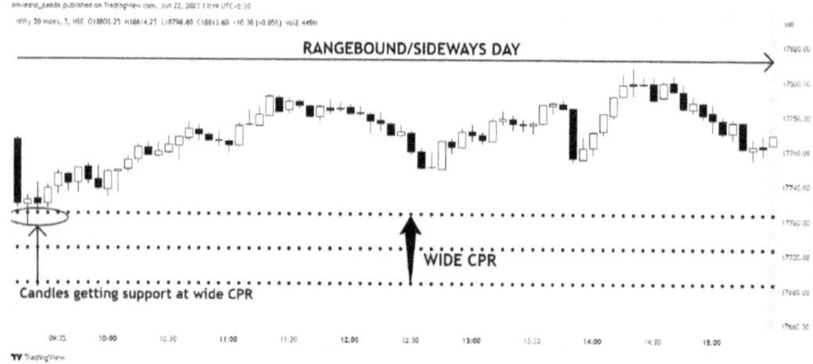

Figure (6.3)

In Figure (6.3), we observe a 5-minute chart of the Nifty 50 Index on April 25, 2023. The chart depicts a notable market scenario where the session commenced with an extremely bearish candle. However, moments later, there was a formation of a bullish pinbar precisely at the wide Central Pivot Range (CPR). This occurrence underscores the significance of wide CPR levels as the candles found immediate support upon touching the CPR. Consequently, there was a noticeable upward momentum in the price action, showcasing how CPR levels can influence market dynamics and signal potential reversals or shifts in sentiment.

Figure (6.4)

Figure (6.4) represents a 5-minute chart of the Nifty Bank Index on June 12, 2023. The chart depicts the market opening with a bearish candle, followed by attempted upward movements that encountered resistance at the wide Central Pivot Range (CPR) not once, but three times. Subsequently, after encountering resistance from the wide CPR on multiple occasions, there was a notable downward momentum in price action. This observation reflects the significance of wide CPR levels as strong resistance zones, influencing market behavior and leading to range-bound price movements. Consequently, the market remained sideways for the entirety of the trading day. This example highlights how traders can use wide CPR levels to identify potential areas of resistance and anticipate market movements accordingly.

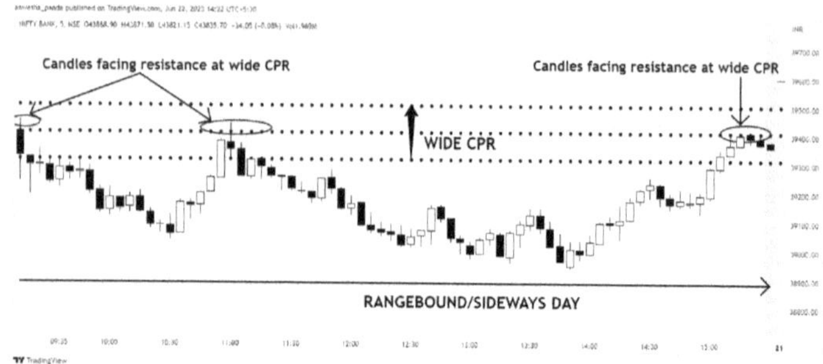

Figure (6.5)

In Figure (6.5), we observe a 5-minute chart of the Nifty Bank Index on March 20, 2023. The chart highlights the market opening with a bearish candle and encountering resistance three times at the wide Central Pivot Range (CPR). Each time the candles attempted upward movements, they faced rejection near the wide CPR, resulting in a downward momentum in price action.

Traders can use such observations to gauge market sentiment and make informed trading decisions based on the behavior around key CPR levels.

NARROW CPR

A narrow Central Pivot Range (CPR) typically serves as weak support and resistance levels in the market. Price movements can easily penetrate through a narrow CPR, making it less powerful compared to a wide CPR. Additionally, a narrow CPR often indicates a potential trending day in the market. Its narrowness gives a strong directional bias, making it a valuable tool for capturing strong and one-sided trending moves. Traders frequently utilize narrow CPR levels to identify and capitalize on significant directional movements in the market, enhancing their ability to participate in trending phases effectively.

Unlike wide CPR levels that act as strong support or resistance, narrow CPR levels signify weaker barriers for price movements. This characteristic allows prices to penetrate through narrow CPR levels relatively easily, limiting their effectiveness as significant price boundaries. However, the significance of a narrow CPR lies in its indication of potential trending market conditions. This can be interpreted as a period in the market, where prices are likely to experience a breakout or strong directional move.

While narrow CPR levels may lack the robustness of wide CPR levels in terms of support and resistance, they offer valuable insights into market sentiment and directional biases. Traders can use narrow CPR levels strategically to catch potential trending moves early in their development. By monitoring price action around narrow CPR boundaries, traders can establish entry points aligned with the anticipated breakout direction.

Figure (6.6)

In Figure (6.6), we examine a 5-minute timeframe chart of the Nifty 50 Index on October 23, 2023. The chart vividly demonstrates how a narrow Central Pivot Range (CPR) can result in a trending trading session. The narrow CPR in this scenario serves as a precursor to a strong and directional market move. Traders can observe how price action interacts with the narrow CPR boundaries, often leading to a breakout or sustained trend in one direction. This observation underscores the importance of monitoring CPR levels, even when they appear narrow, as they can offer valuable insights into potential market trends and trading opportunities.

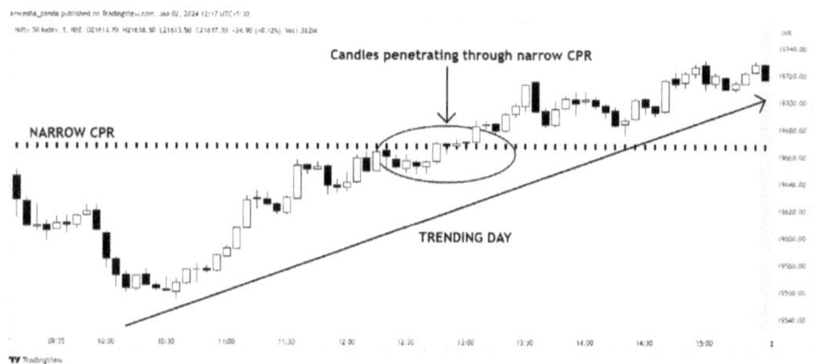

Figure (6.7)

In Figure (6.7), we analyze a 5-minute chart of the Nifty 50 index on September 27, 2023. The chart vividly illustrates how a narrow Central Pivot Range (CPR) functions as a weak resistance level, allowing price movements to penetrate into the CPR boundaries with ease. Unlike wider CPR levels that offer stronger support or resistance, narrow CPR levels lack significant barriers to price movements. By recognizing and leveraging the implications of a narrow CPR, traders can position themselves strategically to capture early stages of trending moves.

VIRGIN CPR

A Virgin Central Pivot Range (CPR) occurs when price levels for a specific timeframe do not touch the CPR levels of the same timeframe during a trading session. This phenomenon indicates a lack of interaction between price movements and the CPR levels on the same trading day. If the candles of a particular trading instrument fail to touch the CPR levels on a given day, it establishes a Virgin CPR for subsequent trading sessions.

If candles breach the Virgin Central Pivot Range (CPR) on a particular day, it loses its status as a Virgin CPR for the following day. Therefore, traders may opt to skip marking it on the chart or considering it as support or resistance levels from the next day onwards. However, when price respects a Virgin CPR, it tends to act as a reliable support or resistance level on the chart.

It's important to note that a wide Virgin Central Pivot Range (CPR) acts as a strong support or resistance level compared to a narrow Virgin CPR.

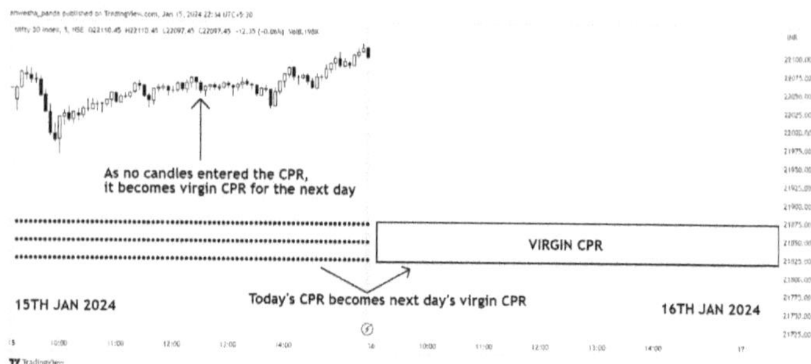

Figure (6.8)

Figure (6.8) displays a 5-minute chart of the Nifty 50 Index on January 15, 2024 and January 16, 2024. Notably, on January 15, 2024, all candles failed to touch the Central Pivot Range (CPR). Throughout the trading hours, the candles consistently traded above the CPR levels and did not enter the CPR boundaries. This price behavior led to the formation of a Virgin CPR on January 16, 2024. The absence of price movement interacting with the CPR levels on January 15, 2024, resulted in the designation of a Virgin CPR for the subsequent trading session on January 16, 2024.

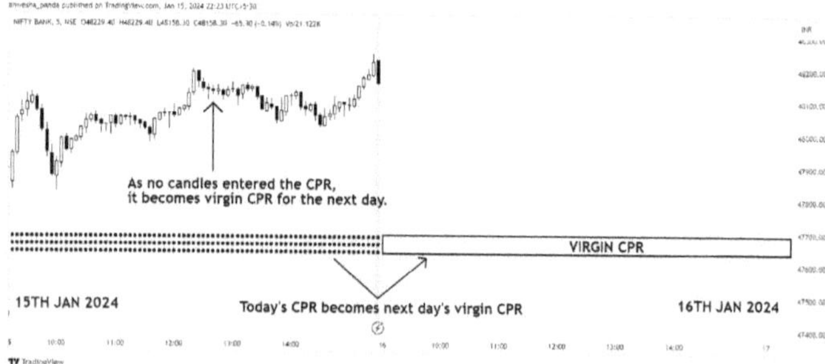

Figure (6.9)

In Figure (6.9), we examine a 5-minute chart of the Nifty Bank Index on January 15, 2024 and January 16, 2024. Notably, on January 15, 2024, none of the candles touched the Central Pivot Range (CPR) levels. Throughout the trading hours, the candles consistently traded above the CPR boundaries, without breaching them. This price action pattern led to the formation of a Virgin CPR on January 16, 2024.

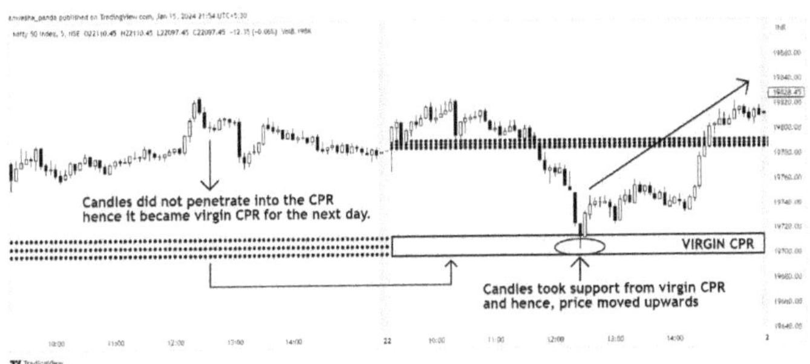

Figure (6.10)

Figure (6.10) illustrates a 5-minute chart of the Nifty 50 Index on November 21, 2023 and November 22, 2023. Notably, on November 21, 2023, none of the candles touched the Central Pivot Range (CPR), leading to the formation of a virgin CPR for the subsequent day. Virgin CPRs are known to act as significant support and resistance levels in trading. On November 22, 2023, the candles indeed found support from the virgin CPR, showcasing its effectiveness as a support level. This support led to an observed upward momentum in price action, culminating in a bullish move.

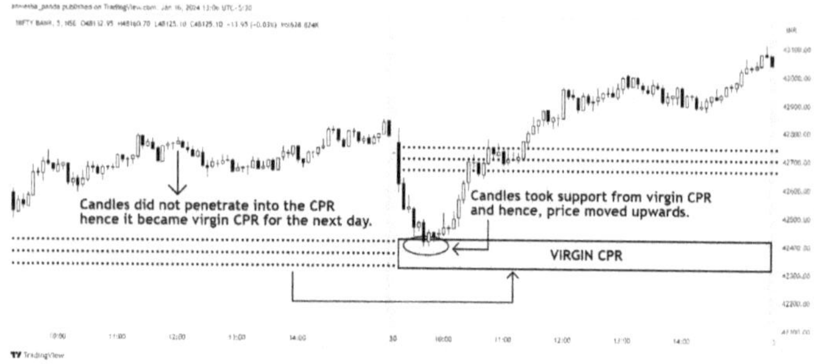

Figure (6.11)

In Figure (6.11), we observe a 5-minute chart of the Nifty Bank Index on October 27, 2023 and October 30, 2023. Notably, on October 27, 2023, none of the candles touched the Central Pivot Range (CPR), leading to the formation of a virgin CPR for the subsequent day. Virgin CPRs are recognized for their role as significant support and resistance levels in trading scenarios. On October 30, 2023, the candles indeed found support from the virgin CPR, highlighting its efficacy as a support level. This support facilitated an observed upward momentum in price action, resulting in a bullish move. Such price behavior underscores the importance of monitoring and acknowledging virgin CPR formations as they can influence market sentiment and guide trading decisions effectively. Traders often use virgin CPR levels as key reference points for identifying potential reversals or continuation of trends, contributing to successful trading strategies.

ASCENDING CPR

When the Central Pivot Range (CPR) consistently forms higher highs every day, it is referred to as an ascending CPR. This pattern indicates a strong uptrend in the price action of a particular trading instrument. Traders keenly observe the formation of an ascending CPR as it suggests favorable conditions for initiating long positions or adopting bullish strategies.

For instance, in Figure (6.12), we can observe the formation of an ascending CPR alongside an uptrend market scenario. Each day, the CPR levels continue to make higher highs, indicating the presence of sustained upward momentum in prices. This pattern reinforces the bullish sentiment in the market, prompting traders to consider buying opportunities or maintaining long positions to capitalize on the uptrend.

Traders who recognize the significance of ascending CPR formations align their trades with the prevailing uptrend, enhancing their chances of profitable outcomes. By monitoring price movements relative to the ascending CPR levels, traders can identify potential entry points for long positions and manage their risk effectively.

In conclusion, understanding the implications of an ascending CPR enables traders to navigate uptrend markets more effectively. By leveraging this pattern to identify long opportunities, traders can enhance their profitability and risk management strategies in bullish market conditions.

Figure (6.12)

RANGEBOUND CPR

When the Central Pivot Range (CPR) forms in a range-bound manner, characterized by fluctuations in the price of a particular trading instrument without exhibiting a clear or sustained trend in either upward or downward direction, it is termed as range-bound CPR. This pattern indicates that the market is moving within a range and lacks a clear directional bias. Traders often encounter range-bound CPR formations during periods of market consolidation or indecision, where prices oscillate within a defined price range without a dominant trend.

For example, in Figure (6.13), we can observe the formation of a range-bound CPR alongside a range-bound or sideways market scenario. During such periods, the CPR levels may act as temporary support and resistance zones within the price range. Traders can use this information to identify potential trading opportunities such as range trading strategies, where they buy near support levels and sell near resistance levels within the established range.

It's important for traders to exercise caution when trading in range-bound markets with range-bound CPR formations. While these patterns lack a clear directional bias, they can still offer profitable trading opportunities if traders effectively identify key support and resistance levels within the range.

Additionally, traders may monitor price action around the CPR levels to anticipate potential breakout or breakdown movements from the range-bound pattern. Breakouts from range-bound CPR formations can signal the start of new trends or extended price movements, offering traders opportunities for trend-following strategies or momentum trading approaches.

In summary, understanding range-bound CPR formations and their implications within range-bound or sideways markets empowers traders to adapt their strategies accordingly. By recognizing key support and resistance levels, monitoring price action, and validating signals with technical analysis, traders can navigate range-bound market conditions effectively and capitalize on trading opportunities within the established price range.

Figure (6.13)

DESCENDING CPR

When observing a market where the Central Pivot Range (CPR) consistently establishes lower lows daily, it reflects the formation of a descending CPR. This pattern indicates a clear downtrend for the particular trading instrument. Traders often look for such signals as they provide valuable insights into potential short-selling opportunities within the market.

For instance, in Figure (6.14), we can discern the formation of a descending CPR alongside a downtrend market scenario. Each day, the CPR continues to make lower lows, highlighting the downward momentum in price action. This pattern reinforces the bearish sentiment in the market, prompting traders to consider creating short positions to capitalize on the anticipated downward movement.

Traders who incorporate descending CPR analysis into their strategies gain a tactical advantage by aligning their trades with the prevailing downtrend. By monitoring how price action interacts with the descending CPR levels, traders can identify optimal entry points for short positions and manage their risk effectively.

In conclusion, understanding the implications of a descending CPR allows traders to navigate downtrend markets more effectively. By leveraging this pattern to identify short-selling opportunities, traders can enhance their profitability and risk management strategies in bearish market conditions.

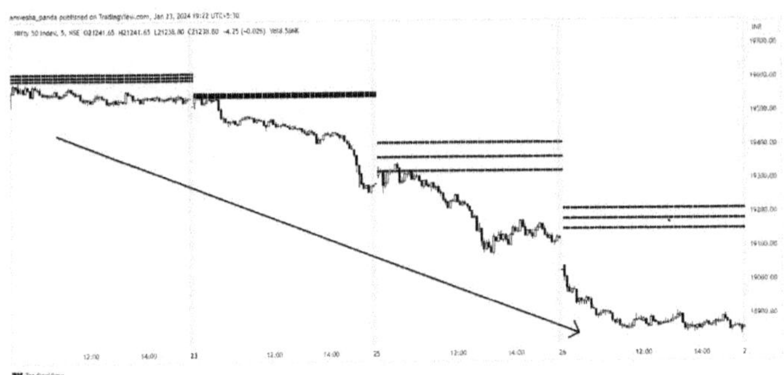

Figure (6.14)

• • •

CHAPTER VII

FORECASTING TREND OF THE MARKET BY ANALYZING THE WIDTH OF CENTRAL PIVOT RANGE (CPR)

While the width of the Central Pivot Range (CPR) itself doesn't forecast trends outright, it does provide valuable insights into potential price levels where market movements might trend or remain sideways. A narrow CPR may suggest a potential for larger price movements, indicating a market that is actively seeking direction. Conversely, a wide CPR might indicate a period of consolidation with no clear directional bias, suggesting a range-bound or sideways market.

In a consolidating or ranging market, the width of the CPR may expand or remain wide, reflecting the lack of a strong directional bias in price movements. On the other hand, a narrow CPR often precedes an expansion in price volatility, leading to trending markets with a clear directional bias in either the upward or downward direction.

Notably, when a wide CPR accompanies range-bound movement in the market on a particular day, traders often anticipate a shift towards a trending and one-sided directional move on the next trading day.

Figure (7.1) displays a 5-minute chart of the Nifty 50 Index on January 11, 2024 and January 12, 2024. On January 11, there was the presence of a wide Central Pivot Range (CPR), indicative of a range-bound trading day. Consequently, we can observe the formation of a narrow

CPR on the following day, leading to a one-sided directional movement in the market.

The wide CPR on January 11, suggested a lack of clear directional bias or significant price movements, as the market traded within a defined range. This range-bound behavior was reflected in the width of the CPR. However, the subsequent formation of a narrow CPR on the next trading day signaled a potential shift in market dynamics. The narrower range indicated reduced volatility and a more focused directional bias, leading to one-sided movement in price action.

Figure (7.1)

Figure (7.2) illustrates a 5-minute chart of the Nifty Bank Index on December 4, 2024 and December 5, 2023. On December 4, there was a narrow Central Pivot Range (CPR), leading to a trending trading session characterized by one-sided bullish movement. Consequently, on the following day, we observe the formation of a wide CPR, indicating range-bound movement in the market.

The narrow CPR on December 4, hinted at reduced volatility and a focused directional bias, contributing to the one-sided bullish movement observed in the price action. Traders often interpret narrow CPR formations as signals of potential trending markets or strong directional biases.

However, the shift to a wide CPR on the subsequent trading day marked a change in market dynamics. The wider range reflected increased volatility or uncertainty, leading to range-bound movement where the price oscillated within a defined range without a clear directional bias.

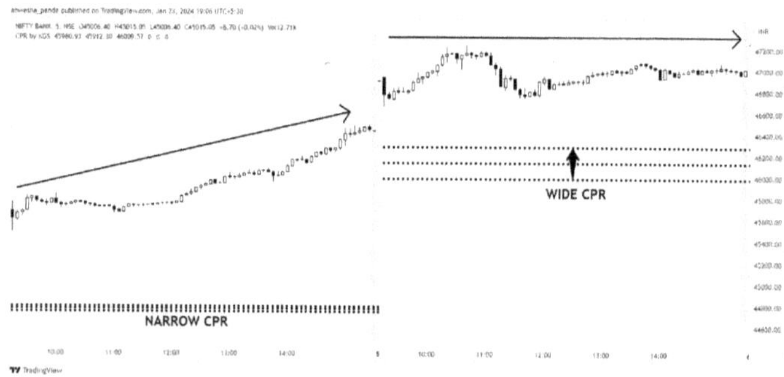

Figure (7.2)

Figure (7.3) provides a detailed view of the 5-minute chart for the Nifty 50 Index, capturing the market movements on March 7, 2024, and March 11, 2024. On March 7, the chart reflects a wide Central Pivot Range (CPR), indicating a market environment where prices oscillated within a relatively broad range without establishing a clear directional bias.

However, the dynamics shifted on the following day, March 11, 2024. Traders observed a significant change as the CPR narrowed, suggesting a decrease in market volatility and a potential shift towards a more focused directional bias.

The wide range of CPR typically implies that the market is consolidating before making a decisive move, offering traders an opportunity to anticipate and position themselves for potential breakout or trend continuation setups.

Figure (7.3)

Figure (7.4) illustrates the 5-minute chart of the Nifty Bank Index on April 5, 2024 and April 8, 2024. On April 5, the chart reveals a narrow Central Pivot Range (CPR), leading to a trending day characterized by a one-sided bullish move. Traders observed strong bullish momentum as the market moved decisively in one direction.

Conversely, on April 8, the chart depicts a wide CPR, indicating a different market scenario. The wider CPR signifies a market that remained sideways or range-bound, lacking a clear directional bias. Traders experienced challenges in identifying a dominant trend or significant price movements as the market exhibited consolidation or indecision during this period.

Figure (7.4)

Understanding the implications of CPR width variations helps traders anticipate shifts in market sentiment and adjust their trading strategies accordingly. Traders may look for breakout opportunities when transitioning from a wide CPR to a narrow CPR, aligning their trades with emerging trends or directional biases in the market. By incorporating this analysis into their trading strategies, traders can adapt to different market conditions, optimize their trade entries and exits, and improve overall trading performance in diverse market environments.

• • •

CHAPTER VIII

BASICS OF PRICE ACTION & IMPORTANT CANDLESTICK PATTERNS

Price action refers to the movement of a financial asset's price as depicted on a chart. It encompasses all the fluctuations in price that occur over a certain period, whether its a chart showing minute-to-minute changes or a chart spanning months or years. Price action analysis involves studying these price movements to make trading decisions. Price action includes open, high, low and close prices for a given timeframe and is often represented through candlestick charts, line charts, bar charts, etc. Analyzing price action involves observing patterns, trends, support and resistance levels, chart formations, and candlestick shapes to anticipate future price movements.

Price action includes the following elements:

1. **Candlestick Patterns:** Price action analysis often involves studying candlestick patterns that display the open, close, high, and low prices for a specific time period. Patterns such as doji, pinbars, engulfing patterns, etc., are interpreted to understand market sentiment.

2. **Support and Resistance Levels:** Traders identify key levels where the price tends to stop rising (resistance) or falling (support). These levels are formed based on historical price movements and play a crucial role in determining potential entry and exit points.

3. **Trends:** Traders analyze trends in the market, such as uptrends, downtrends, or sideways movements. They look for patterns of higher highs and higher lows in an uptrend, lower highs and lower lows in a downtrend, or consolidation in a sideways market.

4. **Chart Patterns:** Traders observe various chart patterns like triangles, flags, head-and-shoulders, etc., to anticipate potential price movements. These patterns often signal continuation or reversal of trends.

5. **Price Action Signals:** Certain price action signals, like pin bars, inside bars, and rejection candles, provide indications of potential reversals or continuations in the market.

Price action is crucial for traders as it provides direct insights into market dynamics and the behavior of buyers and sellers. It is often used by traders to make informed decisions about when to enter or exit trades, manage risk, and understand the overall market sentiment based on the observed price movements and patterns.

CANDLESTICK PATTERNS

Candlestick patterns are graphical representations of price movements for financial assets displayed on a chart over a specific period. They are formed by candlesticks which illustrate the open, high, low, and close prices for a given timeframe (e.g: minutes, hours, days).

Each candlestick consists of two main parts:

1. **Body:** The rectangular part of the candlestick represents the price range between the opening and closing prices during the selected timeframe. If the closing price is

higher than the opening price, the body is typically filled or colored, often green or white, indicating a bullish (positive) movement. Conversely, if the closing price is lower than the opening price, the body is often empty or colored red or black, signifying a bearish (negative) movement.

2. **Wicks or Shadows:** The thin lines, known as wicks or shadows, extend above and below the body of the candlestick. These lines display the highest and lowest prices reached during the selected timeframe. The upper wick indicates the highest price, while the lower wick shows the lowest price.

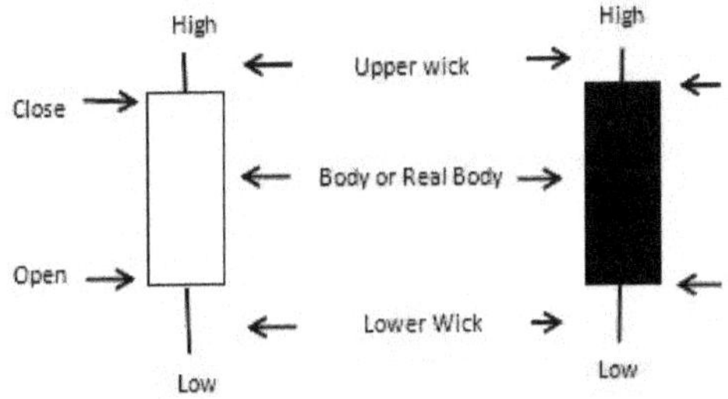

Figure (8.1)

Candlestick patterns are formed by multiple candlesticks in specific arrangements and sequences. These patterns help traders interpret market sentiment and potential future price movements. Some common candlestick patterns include:

DOJI

A doji is a candlestick pattern that forms when the opening and closing prices of an asset are very close to or virtually the same, resulting in a very small or non-existent body. It appears as a cross, a plus sign, or a horizontal line with little to no vertical length.

Key characteristics of a doji include:

- **Small or Non-existent Body:** The open and close prices are extremely close or identical, creating a small or non-existent body for the candlestick.
- **Long Upper and Lower Wicks:**Doji candles typically have long upper and lower wicks that extend beyond the body. These wicks represent the highest and lowest prices reached during the timeframe.
- **Indication of Market Indecision:**A doji suggests a temporary standoff between buyers and sellers, where neither side has managed to establish control over the price. It often forms during periods of market indecision or when the market sentiment is uncertain.

Doji candlesticks are considered significant because they represent a balance between buyers and sellers, potentially signaling a reversal or a period of consolidation in the market. Depending on where they occur in a price chart and in what context, doji candles can indicate potential trend reversals if they appear after a prolonged uptrend or downtrend. They can also signal a continuation of the current trend if they occur within a consolidation phase.

Traders often interpret doji candles as a potential opportunity for a change in market sentiment and may use them as part of their analysis when making trading decisions. However, it's essential to consider the overall market context to confirm the significance of a doji pattern before taking any trading actions.

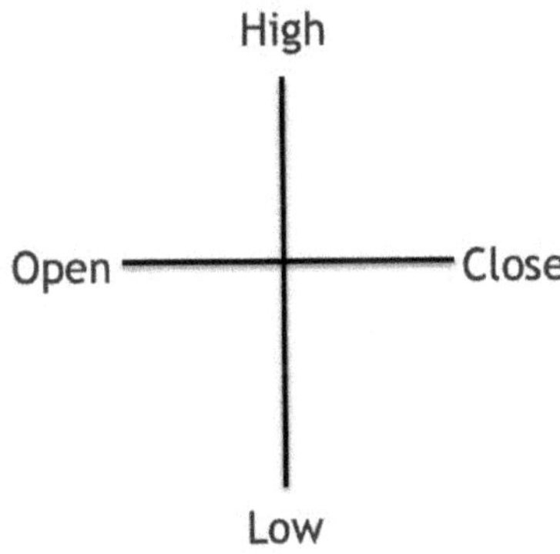

Figure (8.2)

BULLISH PINBAR

A bullish pin bar is a candlestick pattern that typically forms at the bottom of a downtrend and suggests a potential reversal in price direction from bearish to bullish. It consists of three main parts:

- **Long Lower Wick:** The lower wick (also called the tail or shadow) is longer than the upper wick. It represents the lowest price reached during the period, indicating that sellers pushed the price significantly lower but failed to maintain it at that level.

- **Small Body:** The body of the candlestick is relatively small and is located at the top of the entire candle. It can be green or white, but its size is comparatively smaller than the length of the lower wick.
- **Short Upper Wick:**The upper wick is shorter and represents the highest price reached during the period. It indicates that buyers attempted to push the price higher but were unable to sustain it at those levels. It may or may not be present.

A bullish pin bar suggests a potential shift from a downtrend to an uptrend. The long lower wick shows that sellers were strong initially but failed to keep the price low, while the small body and short upper wick indicate that buyers stepped in and managed to push the price higher by the end of the period.

The bullish pin bar is often seen as a signal to consider going long (buying) on the asset because it signifies a possible change in market sentiment from bearishness to bullishness. However, as with any candlestick pattern, it's important to use additional confirmation signals and consider the overall market context before making trading decisions.

BEARISH PINBAR

A bearish pin bar is a candlestick pattern that typically forms at the top of an uptrend and signals a potential reversal from bullish to bearish. It comprises three main components:

- **Long Upper Wick:**The upper wick (also known as the tail or shadow) is longer than the lower wick. It represents the highest price reached during the period, indicating that buyers initially pushed the price higher but failed to sustain it at those levels.
- **Small Body:** The body of the candlestick is relatively small and is positioned at the bottom of the entire candle. It can be either red or black, but its size is comparatively smaller than the length of the upper wick.
- **Short Lower Wick:** The lower wick is shorter and signifies the lowest price reached during the period. It indicates that sellers attempted to push the price lower but were unable to maintain it at those levels. It may or maynot be present.

The bearish pin bar suggests a potential shift from an uptrend to a downtrend. The long upper wick demonstrates that buyers initially had control but failed to sustain the higher prices. Meanwhile, the small body and short lower wick indicate that sellers managed to push the price down by the end of the period.

The bearish pin bar is often seen as a signal to consider short positions (selling) on the asset, as it indicates a potential change in market sentiment from bullishness to bearishness. However, it's essential to confirm this pattern with additional signals and consider the broader market context before making trading decisions.

Figure (8.3)

BULLISH ENGULFING PATTERN

A bullish engulfing pattern is a two-candlestick reversal pattern that often occurs at the end of a downtrend. It signifies a potential shift from a bearish to a bullish market sentiment. This pattern consists of two candles:

- **Bearish Candlestick:** The first candlestick is a bearish (downward) candle, signaling the continuation of the downtrend. It has a larger body and sets the tone for the pattern.
- **Bullish Candlestick:** The second candlestick is a bullish (upward) candle that completely engulfs the body of the preceding bearish candle. The bullish candle's body is typically larger than the body of the bearish candle.

Key features of a bullish engulfing pattern:

1. The bullish candle's body completely covers or engulfs the entire body of the previous bearish candle, including its shadows or wicks.
2. The bullish candle opens lower than the previous candle's low and closes higher than the previous candle's high.
3. The pattern suggests a shift in momentum from bearishness to bullishness, indicating potential buying pressure overcoming the selling pressure.
4. The bullish engulfing pattern is considered a strong bullish signal by traders as it demonstrates a significant change in market sentiment. It implies that buyers have gained control and are overpowering the sellers, potentially leading to a reversal or the beginning of an uptrend.
5. Traders often use the bullish engulfing pattern as a signal to enter long (buy) positions or as confirmation of a potential trend reversal. However, it's essential to consider other technical indicators, market conditions, and the overall context before making trading decisions solely based on this pattern.

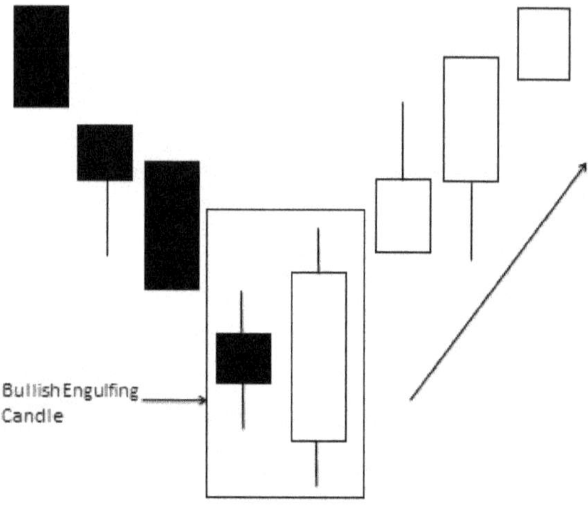

Figure (8.4)

BEARISH ENGULFING PATTERN

The bearish engulfing pattern is a significant two-candlestick reversal pattern commonly observed at the end of an uptrend. It signifies a potential shift in market sentiment from bullish to bearish, indicating a possible reversal or downtrend in price action. This pattern consists of two candles:

- **Bullish Candlestick:** The first candlestick is bullish (upward), reflecting ongoing upward price momentum in the market. It typically has a smaller body compared to the second candle.

- **Bearish Candlestick:** The second candlestick is bearish (downward) and completely engulfs the body of the preceding bullish candle. Its body is usually larger than that of the bullish candle.

Key features of a bearish engulfing pattern:

1. The bearish candle's body completely covers or engulfs the entire body of the previous bullish candle, including its shadows or wicks.
2. The bearish candle opens higher than the previous candle's high and closes lower than the previous candle's low.
3. The pattern suggests a shift in momentum from bullishness to bearishness, indicating potential selling pressure overpowering buying pressure.
4. Traders interpret the bearish engulfing pattern as a strong bearish signal, suggesting a potential reversal or the beginning of a downtrend. It implies that sellers have gained control, potentially leading to lower prices.
5. Traders often use this pattern as a signal to enter short (sell) positions or as confirmation of a potential trend reversal. However, it's important to confirm the pattern with other technical indicators and consider market conditions before making trading decisions solely based on this pattern.

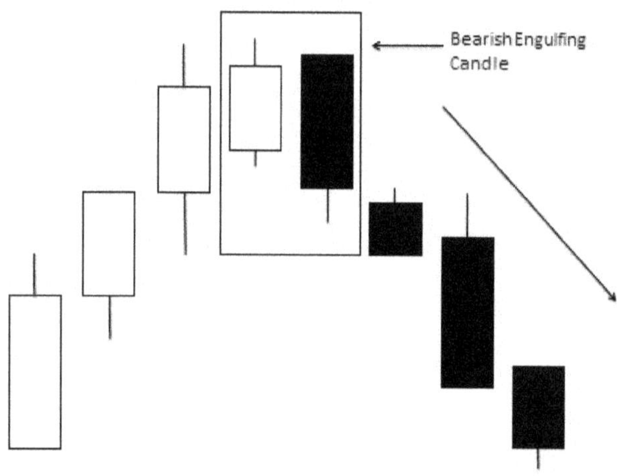

Figure (8.5)

MORNING STAR

The Morning Star is a bullish candlestick pattern that typically occurs at the end of a downtrend and signals a potential reversal in the market direction from bearish to bullish. It's composed of three candlesticks and is considered a strong indicator of a potential change in market sentiment. Here's how the Morning Star pattern is formed:

- **First Candlestick:** The pattern begins with a long bearish (downward) candlestick, reflecting the prevailing downtrend.
- **Second Candlestick:**The second candlestick appears as a small-bodied candle, often a doji or a small bullish

candle, and signifies indecision or a slowdown in the downtrend. This candlestick gap is present between the first and third candles.

- **Third Candlestick:** The third candlestick is a strong bullish (upward) candlestick that closes well into the body of the first bearish candle. It indicates a shift in momentum from bearishness to bullishness, with significant buying pressure.

Key aspects of the Morning Star pattern:

1. The first candlestick is bearish and reflects the continuation of the downtrend.
2. The second candlestick is smaller and shows a potential weakening of the bearish momentum or market indecision.
3. The third candlestick is a strong bullish candle that closes well within the range of the first candle, signaling a possible reversal to an uptrend.

The Morning Star pattern is considered a reliable bullish signal by traders as it suggests that buyers are gaining control and a reversal in the downtrend may be imminent. However, as with any technical analysis tool, it's important to confirm this pattern with other indicators or signals and consider the broader market context before making trading decisions based solely on the morning Star pattern.

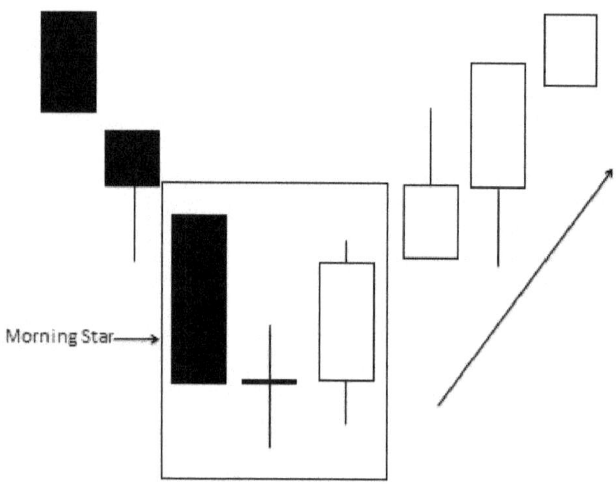

Figure (8.6)

EVENING STAR PATTERN

The Evening Star is a bearish candlestick pattern that often signals a potential reversal from an uptrend to a downtrend in the market. It consists of three candles and typically appears on price charts. Here's how the Evening Star pattern forms:

- **First Candle:**The pattern begins with a large bullish (upward) candlestick, representing the prevailing uptrend.
- **Second Candle:** Following the bullish candle, there is a small-bodied candlestick (either a doji or a small

bullish/bearish candle) that indicates indecision or a potential weakening of the bullish momentum. This candle may also have small upper and lower shadows.

- **Third Candle:**The third candle is a strong bearish (downward) candlestick that closes well below the midpoint of the first bullish candle's body. This bearish candle confirms the potential reversal and demonstrates significant selling pressure, indicating a shift in sentiment from bullishness to bearishness.

Key characteristics of the Evening Star pattern:

1. The first candle is bullish, reflecting the existing uptrend.
2. The second candle shows indecision or a potential weakening of the uptrend.
3. The third candle is a strong bearish candle that closes well into the body of the first candle, suggesting a reversal and bearish momentum.

The Evening Star pattern is considered a reliable bearish reversal signal by traders as it implies a change in market sentiment from bullish to bearish. It indicates that sellers are gaining strength and are likely to take control of the market.

Evening Star pattern is often seen as an opportunity to enter short (sell) positions or as confirmation of a potential trend reversal. However, as with any candlestick pattern, it's important to consider other technical indicators, market conditions, and the overall context before making trading decisions solely based on this pattern.

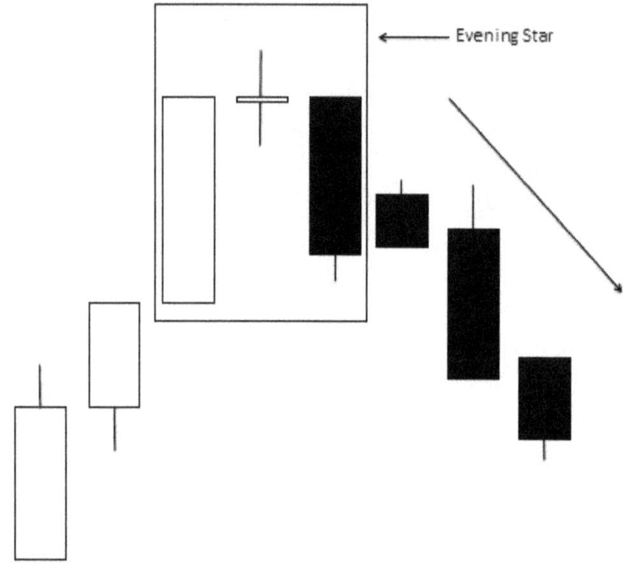

Figure (8.7)

SUPPORT AND RESISTANCE

Support is a price level or a zone where the price of an asset tends to stop falling further or encounters buying interest. It's a level that historically shows a tendency for the price to bounce back up after reaching that point. Traders view support levels as areas where there's a perceived value in buying an asset because it is deemed undervalued or attractive at that price, leading to an increase in buying pressure.

Resistance is the opposite of support. It represents a price level or zone where the price tends to stop rising or encounters selling pressure. It's a level where historically, the price struggles to break through and continues its upward movement. Traders view resistance levels as areas where selling interest increases, leading to a potential halt or reversal in the price's upward momentum.

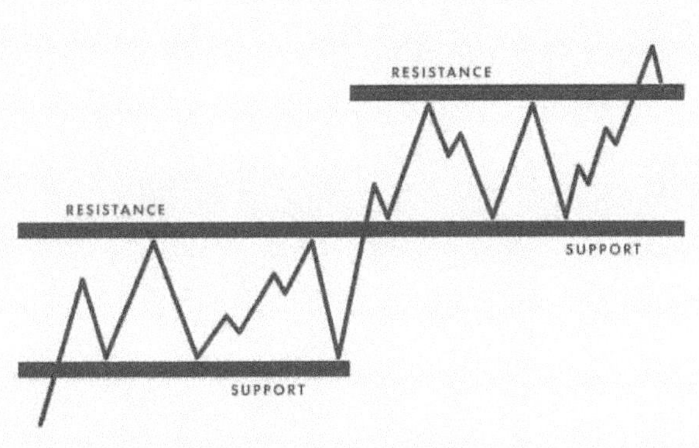

Figure (8.8)

Support turning into Resistance: If a support level is broken decisively, it might act as a resistance level in the future. Once the price falls below a support level, that level often becomes a barrier for upward movement, as previous buyers might now become sellers at that level.

Resistance turning into Support: If a resistance level is breached, it might transform into a support level. Once the price rises above a resistance level, that level might act as a support for future price movements, as previous sellers might now become buyers at that level.

• • •

CHAPTER IX

INTRADAY TRADING STRATEGIES FOR NIFTY & NIFTY BANK

In the dynamic realm of financial markets, few indices command the attention and interest of traders as much as Nifty and Nifty Bank. These benchmarks, renowned for their reflection of the Indian stock market, stand as pillars influencing investor sentiment, economic forecasts, and trading strategies. In the upcoming sections, we will delve into strategies that adapt to volatility, capitalize on trends, and navigate the uncertainties that often define these indices. However, beyond trading techniques, the subsequent chapters aim to foster a mindset—one that values discipline, embraces risk management, and prioritizes continuous learning as the cornerstones of successful trading endeavors.

It's essential to remember that while CPR and its unique characteristics offer valuable insights, it's equally crucial to consider the broader market context, including news events, economic data, and other factors impacting price movements. Using CPR as part of a comprehensive strategy, rather than relying solely on it for trading decisions, is a prudent approach. Always practice risk management and consider multiple factors before executing trades based solely on CPR or any single indicator.

Trading in indices like Nifty and Nifty Bank demands a blend of discipline, adaptability, and a deep understanding of market dynamics. While there's no universal strategy, success comes from integrating multiple strategies and maintaining a keen awareness of market intricacies. This holistic approach is fundamental to thriving in the ever-evolving landscape of index trading.

• • •

CHAPTER X

TRADING IN RANGEBOUND MARKETS AFTER A HUGE TRENDING DAY USING CPR

After a significant trending day, there's a high likelihood that the market will consolidate into a rangebound state the following day. Figure (10.1) depicts the Nifty chart for October 10, 2023 and October 11, 2023, illustrating a sharp and trending session on October 10, followed by a sideways market on October 11. The chart showcases a narrow Central Pivot Range (CPR) on October 10 and a wider CPR on October 11. This transition from a narrow to a wider CPR aligns with the expected shift from a trending to a rangebound market scenario, reflecting the market's tendency to consolidate after a significant directional move.

Figure (10.1)

Figure (10.2) depicts the chart of the Nifty 50 Index on September 11, 2023 and September 12, 2023. September 11 unfolded as a clear trending day, characterized by a discernible directional bias in the market. However, on September 12, the market lacked a proper directional bias, resulting in a range-bound trading session. The chart further illustrates a narrow CPR on September 11 and a wider CPR on September 12. This transition from a narrow to a wider CPR mirrors the shift from a trending to a range-bound market environment, reflecting the market's tendency to consolidate following a significant directional move.

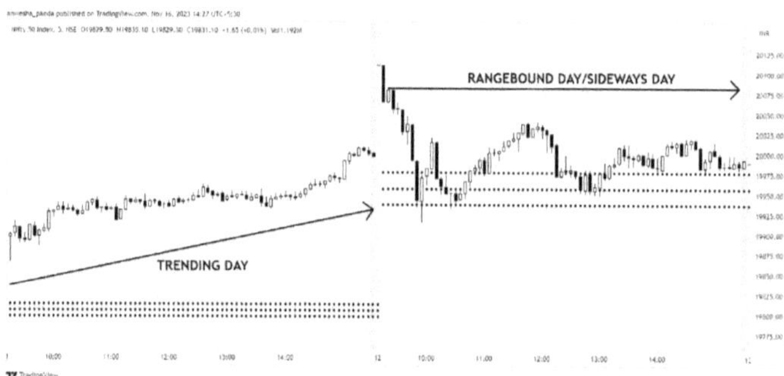

Figure (10.2)

Figure (10.3) illustrates the chart of the Nifty Bank Index on August 28, 2023 and August 29, 2023. August 28 displayed a clear trending day characterized by a distinct directional bias in the market. Conversely, August 29 unfolded as a range-bound day, where the market lacked a clear directional bias and traded within a defined range.

Figure (10.3)

Wide CPR typically acts as strong support and resistance levels, whereas narrow CPR tends to act as weaker support and resistance levels. In Figure (10.4), we observe the 5-minute chart of August 29, 2023, for the Nifty Bank Index, which was a range-bound day. The wide CPR indicated a strong support area. As the market moved downward after breaking the previous day's high, it formed a bullish harami pattern near the CPR. Consequently, the price found support at the CPR and moved upward, indicating a positive bullish momentum.

Traders could have considered a long position when the Nifty Bank Index formed a bullish harami at the CPR, understanding that it was a rangebound market day and the wide CPR would likely act as strong support. Profits could have been taken at the Previous Day High (PDH) or at a multiple of the risk taken (2R), with a stop loss placed below the Bullish Harami candle. This example highlights the importance of combining technical analysis with an understanding of market context to identify favorable trading opportunities and manage risk prudently.

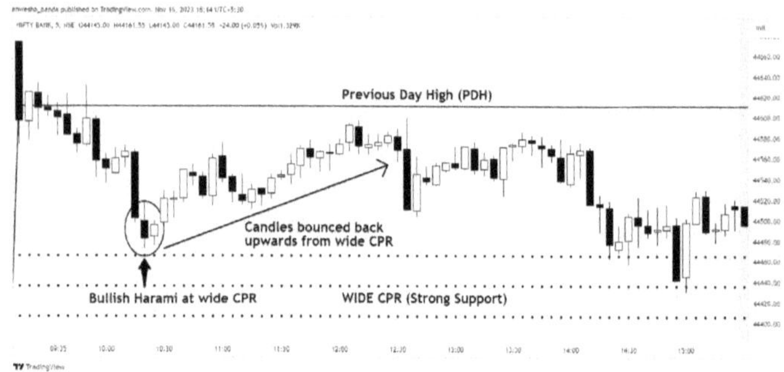

Figure (10.4)

Figure (10.5) illustrates the chart of the Nifty 50 Index on December 15, 2023 and December 18, 2023. December 15 unfolded as a clear trending day, characterized by significant directional movement in the market. In contrast, December 18 is a range-bound day, where the market lacks a clear directional bias and trades within a defined range.

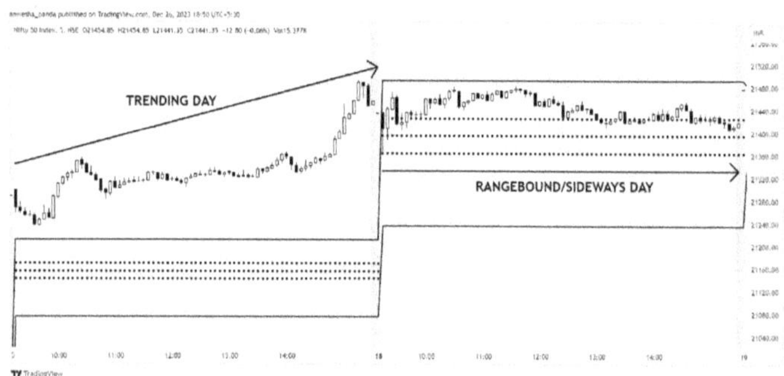

Figure (10.5)

In Figure (10.6), we observe the 5-minute chart of December 18, 2023, in the Nifty 50 Index, which represents a range-bound market day. The wide CPR indicates a robust support area. When the market formed a bullish pinbar candle near the CPR, it signaled a potential reversal, and the price found support at the CPR, subsequently moving upwards.

Traders could have taken advantage of this setup by initiating long positions when Nifty formed a bullish pinbar at the CPR, considering the range-bound nature of the market for that day and the strong support offered by the wide CPR. Profit-taking opportunities could have been sought near the Previous Day High (PDH) or at 1:2 risk-reward ratio. To manage risk effectively, a stop-loss order could have been placed below the bullish pinbar candle.

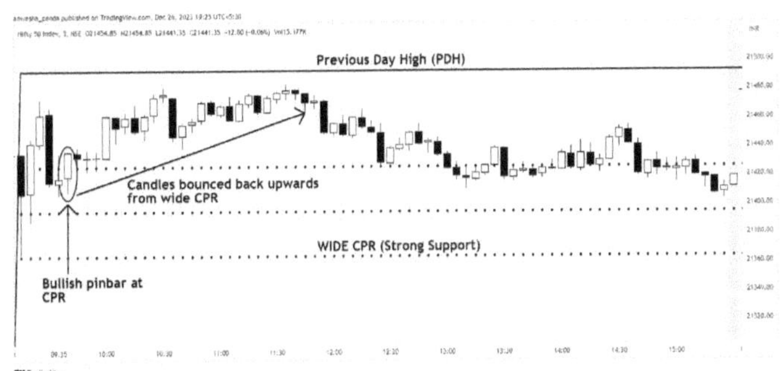

Figure (10.6)

Figure (10.7) illustrates the chart of the Nifty Bank Index on December 12, 2023 and December 13, 2023. December 12 unfolded as a clear trending day, characterized by significant directional movement in the market. However, on December 13, the market shifted to a range-bound state, lacking a clear directional bias and trading within a defined range.

Figure (10.7)

In Figure (10.8), depicting the 5-minute chart of December 13, 2023, in the Nifty Bank Index, we observe a range-bound trading day. The wide CPR indicates a strong resistance area. As the market moved downwards after forming a significant bearish candle near the CPR, the price encountered resistance at the CPR and moved downward.

Traders could have taken advantage of this setup by entering short positions when the Nifty Bank Index formed bearish candles at the CPR, recognizing the range-bound nature of the market that day and understanding the wide CPR's potential as a strong resistance level. Profits could have been taken at the Previous Day Low (PDL) or at 1:2 risk-reward ratio. A stop loss could have been placed above the bearish candles to manage risk effectively.

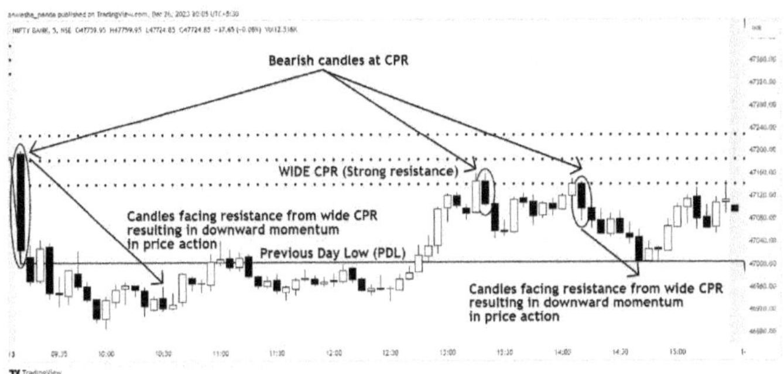

Figure (10.8)

Figure (10.9) illustrates the chart of the Nifty Bank Index on October 18, 2023 and October 19, 2023. October 18 unfolded as a clear trending day, characterized by significant directional movement in the market. However, on October 19, the market transitioned to a range-bound state, lacking a clear directional bias and trading within a defined range.

Figure (10.9)

In Figure (10.10), depicting the 5-minute chart of October 19, 2023, in the Nifty Bank Index, we observe a range-bound market day. The wide CPR indicates a strong resistance area. As the market moved downwards after forming bearish pinbars near the CPR, traders could have taken advantage of this setup by entering short positions. Recognizing the range-bound nature of the market that day and understanding the wide CPR's potential as a strong resistance level, traders could have aimed for profits at the Previous Day Low (PDL) or at 1:2 risk-reward ratio. Managing risk effectively, a stop-loss could have been placed above the bearish pinbar candles.

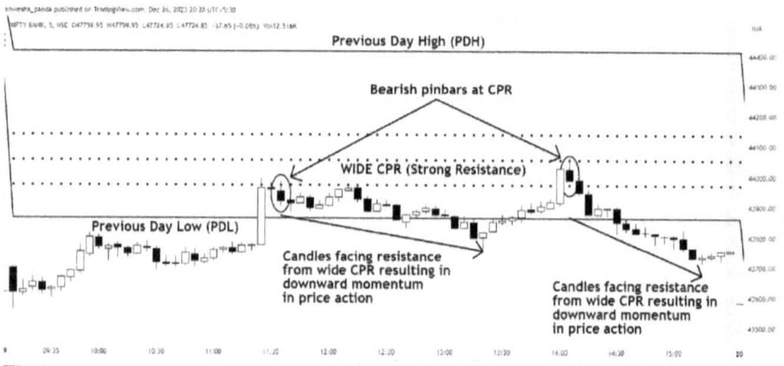

Figure (10.10)

CHAPTER XI

IDENTIFYING PRICE REJECTIONS USING PIVOTS & 200 EMA

In the preceding chapters, we delved into the concept of pivots and explored their application in trading. In this chapter, we will explore the significance of 200 EMA and pivots, as well as learn about their practical utilization in trading strategies. Before delving into various charts, let's familiarize ourselves with the characteristic features of 200 EMA. Additionally, we will learn about its application and relevance in the Indian financial markets.

WHAT IS 200 EMA ?

200 EMA refers to the 200-period Exponential Moving Average, a widely popular technical analysis tool used in financial markets for trading and investment purposes. It is calculated by taking the average closing prices of an asset over the past 200 periods, giving more weight to recent prices through exponential calculation.

Exponential Moving Average (EMA) is different from Simple Moving Average (SMA). EMA places more emphasis on the most recent data points, making it more responsive to price changes. Traders often use 200 EMA to determine the trend in the market. For instance, when the price of an asset is above 200 EMA, it might be considered in an uptrend, while trading below it might indicate a downtrend. It is a valuable tool for analyzing trends and potential support and resistance levels in the market.

IMPORTANCE OF 200 EMA

- **Trend identification:** It helps in identifying the long-term trend of a security. If the price is above 200 EMA, it's often considered bullish, while trading below it could signal a bearish trend.
- **Support and resistance:** 200 EMA often acts as a dynamic support or resistance level. When prices approach this average, one can often look for potential reversals or bounces.
- **Confirmation of trends:** 200 EMA can be used to confirm whether a trend is strong or weakening. For instance, if the price makes a pullback to the 200 EMA and holds as support, it could reinforce the strength of the current trend.
- **Long-term market sentiment:** As it is calculated using a significant number of periods (200 in this case), the 200 EMA reflects long-term market sentiments. Many traders, investors, and institutions pay attention to this moving average for insights into the broader market direction.

Below are a few examples of charts illustrating instances of price rejection in the Nifty 50 and Nifty Bank indices, identified through the use of pivot points and the 200-day exponential moving average (EMA).

Figure (11.1)

Figure (11.1) depicts the 5-minute chart of the Nifty Bank Index onOctober 19, 2023. The market exhibited an upward trend in the first half of the day followed by a period of sideways movement for the remainder of the session. In the latter half of the day, a bearish pinbar was formed at the intersection of the Central Pivot Range (CPR) and the 200-day Exponential Moving Average (EMA). The clustering of multiple resistance levels at a single point creates a challenging scenario for the market to overcome all resistances, hindering the possibility of any significant positive momentum.

The formation of a bearish pinbar at the confluence of the CPR and the 200-day exponential moving average (EMA) signifies a strong rejection of higher prices in that area. This scenario suggests an opportunity to enter a short position, with potential profit-taking targets set at 1:2 risk-reward ratio or based on one's risk tolerance level. Following the rejection of candles at a strong resistance level, there was a subsequent downward momentum in price action, resulting in a rally of over 200 points.

Figure (11.2)

Figure (11.2) illustrates the 5-minute chart of the Nifty Bank Index on October 16, 2023. The market initiated an upward movement during the first half of the day, breaking the previous day's low and demonstrating a strong positive momentum towards the CPR. During the latter half of the day, bearish rejection candles formed at the intersection of the CPR and the 200-day exponential moving average (EMA). The presence of multiple resistances in one area creates a strong barrier for the market to overcome, hindering the potential for any positive momentum.

The formation of bearish candles at the confluence of the Central Pivot Range (CPR) and the 200-day Exponential Moving Average (EMA) signals a significant rejection of higher prices in that region, indicating a potential opportunity to enter a short position and consider profit-taking at a 1:2 risk-reward ratio or in line with one's risk tolerance. Following the rejection of candles at a strong resistance level, we observed a downward momentum in price action, which ultimately led to a rally of over 200 points.

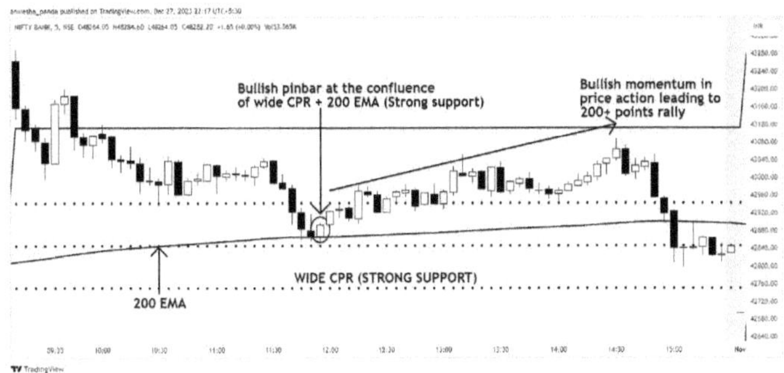

Figure (11.3)

Figure (11.3) illustrates the 5-minute chart of the Nifty Bank Index on October 31, 2023. The market began moving downwards in the first half of the day. In the latter half, a bullish pinbar formed at the confluence of the CPR and the 200-day exponential moving average (EMA). The accumulation of numerous supports in a single area poses a challenge for the market to breach all supports and show any kind of negative momentum.

The formation of a bullish pin bar at the confluence of the Central Pivot Range (CPR) and the 200 EMA suggests a strong rejection of lower prices in that area, potentially signaling an opportunity to enter a long position, with profit-taking at a 1:2 risk-reward ratio or according to one's risk tolerance. Following a strong bounce off the confluence of the Central Pivot Range (CPR) and the 200-day Exponential Moving Average (EMA), we witnessed a significant uptick in price momentum, culminating in a rally of over 200 points.

Figure (11.4)

Figure (11.4) depicts the 5-minute chart of the Nifty Bank Index on February 1, 2024. During the latter half of the trading day, a bullish candle formed at the intersection of the Central Pivot Range (CPR) and the 200-day Exponential Moving Average (EMA). The clustering of multiple support levels at this juncture posed challenges for downward momentum to gain traction, hindering significant downward movement in prices.

The emergence of a bullish candle at the confluence of the Central Pivot Range (CPR) and the 200-day Exponential Moving Average (EMA) suggests a strong rejection of lower price levels, potentially signaling an opportunity to enter a long position. Traders may consider capitalizing on this setup, aiming to secure profits at a 1:2 risk-reward ratio or according to their individual risk tolerance levels.

Following the rejection indicated by strong resistance, we observed an upward shift in price action with reduced downward pressure. This price behavior aligns with the notion that the confluence of key technical levels can influence market sentiment and offer strategic entry points for traders.

. . .

CHAPTER XII

CPR REVERSAL STRATEGY

In trading, CPR (Central Pivot Range) can indeed act as a significant support and resistance level, often signaling potential reversals in price movements. Monitoring price action around these CPR levels alongside other technical indicators can provide valuable insights into market sentiment and potential trading opportunities.

Figure (12.1) presents a detailed 5-minute chart capturing the trading activity of the Nifty 50 Index on November 28, 2023. As we examine the chart, we notice a compelling pattern unfold: after a brief period of downward movement, the market experiences a notable shift as a bullish candlestick pattern forms precisely at or near the CPR level. This event is significant because it signals a strategic reversal point where market participants recognize the support offered by the CPR and take action accordingly.

The impact of this support becomes evident in the subsequent positive momentum in price action, leading to a substantial upward rally. This sequence of events highlights the CPR's role not only in supporting declining prices but also in catalyzing market sentiment shifts that favor upward movements.

Traders and analysts closely monitor these interactions with the CPR, leveraging such insights to make informed trading decisions. Understanding the CPR's influence can help traders identify strategic entry and exit points, manage risk more effectively, and capitalize on emerging market trends.

In essence, Figure (12.1) serves as a compelling case study showcasing the practical application of technical analysis, particularly the role of the CPR as a potent support level in guiding market movements. By recognizing and leveraging these critical levels, traders can navigate market volatility with greater confidence and precision, ultimately enhancing their trading strategies and outcomes.

Figure (12.1)

Figure (12.2) portrays a 5-minute chart of the Nifty 50 Index on October 23, 2023. This chart vividly illustrates how the Central Pivot Range (CPR) operates as a potent resistance level, actively rejecting candles that come into contact with it. This rejection of higher prices sets the stage for a pronounced bearish move in the market. Following a brief period of range-bound movement, the chart reveals the formation of bearish candles precisely on or near the CPR levels.

The CPR's ability to provide formidable resistance becomes evident as it consistently repels higher prices. This resistance contributes significantly to the negative momentum observed in price action, ultimately culminating in a substantial downward rally.

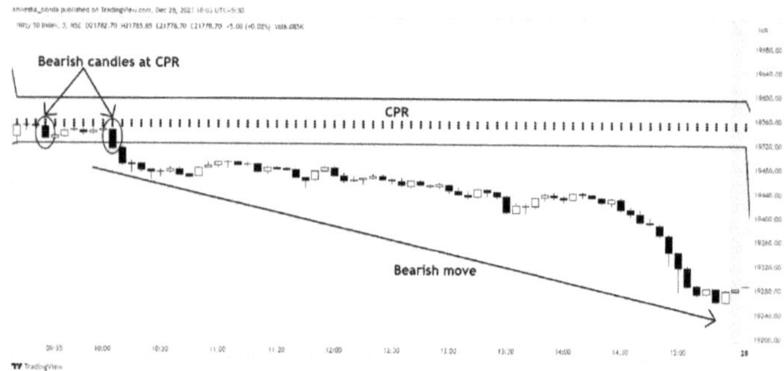

Figure (12.2)

Figure (12.3) portrays a 5-minute chart of the Nifty 50 Index on October 25, 2023. This figure illustrates how the Central Pivot Range (CPR) functions as a potent resistance, resulting in the rejection of candles that touch the CPR, subsequently leading to a significant bearish move as higher prices are turned away. Following a brief period of range-bound movement, the formation of bearish candles or patterns on the CPR becomes evident. The CPR's effective resistance is highlighted, contributing to negative momentum in price action and ultimately triggering a substantial downward rally.

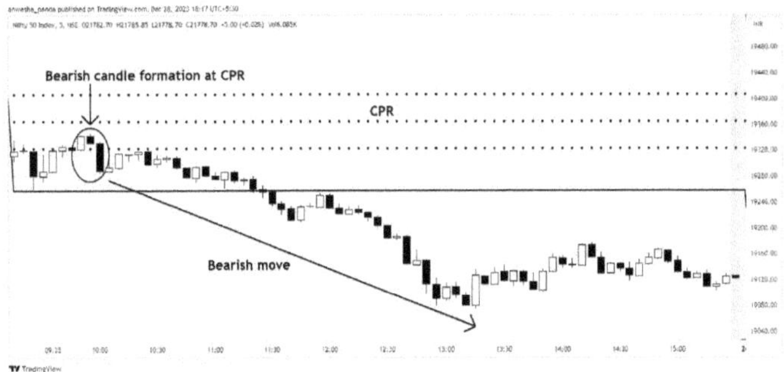

Figure (12.3)

Figure (12.4) illustrates a 5-minute chart of the Nifty Bank Index on October 25, 2023. This figure demonstrates how the Central Pivot Range (CPR) functions as a potent resistance, resulting in the rejection of candles that touch the CPR, subsequently leading to a significant bearish move as higher prices are turned away. Following a brief period of range-bound movement, the formation of bearish candles on the CPR becomes evident. The CPR's effective resistance is highlighted, contributing to negative momentum in price action and ultimately triggering a substantial downward rally.

Figure (12.4)

Figure (12.5) represents a 5-minute chart of the Nifty Bank Index on September 29, 2023. This figure depicts how the CPR acts as a powerful support, providing assistance to the candles that touch the CPR. Subsequently, lower prices were rejected, leading to a significant bullish move. Following a brief period of downward movement, we observe the formation of a bullish pinbar candle on the CPR. The CPR effectively supported the declining prices, resulting in a positive momentum in price action and triggering a substantial upward rally.

Figure (12.5)

Figure (12.6) showcases a 5-minute chart of the Nifty Bank Index on February 15, 2024, effectively demonstrating the role of the Central Pivot Range (CPR) as a robust support level. The chart vividly illustrates how the CPR provides crucial assistance to candles that come into contact with it, subsequently leading to the rejection of lower prices and instigating a notable bullish move in the market.

After a brief period of downward movement, the chart reveals the emergence of a bullish pinbar candle precisely on or near the CPR level. This event underscores the CPR's efficacy in supporting declining prices, thereby generating positive momentum in price action and sparking a substantial upward rally. This depiction serves as a compelling example of how the CPR functions as a reliable support level in technical analysis.

Figure (12.6)

Figure (12.7) depicts a 5-minute chart of the Nifty Bank Index on January 24, 2024, highlighting the role of the Central Pivot Range (CPR) as a strong resistance level. The figure illustrates how the CPR functions by rejecting candles that touch it, leading to a significant bearish move as higher prices are repelled.

After a brief period of bullish momentum, as the candles approached the CPR, there was a formation of bearish candles. This occurrence underscores the CPR's effective resistance, contributing to negative momentum in price action and ultimately initiating a substantial downward rally.

When the price approaches the CPR and encounters resistance, traders may consider initiating short positions or selling trades. This strategy anticipates a continuation of the bearish momentum initiated by the rejection at the CPR. Traders can set stop-loss orders above the CPR to manage risk in case the price breaks through the resistance level. Traders can wait for confirmation signals such as bearish candlestick patterns or technical indicators aligning with the CPR resistance. These signals can strengthen the conviction in taking short positions or exiting long positions, reinforcing the expected downward price movement.

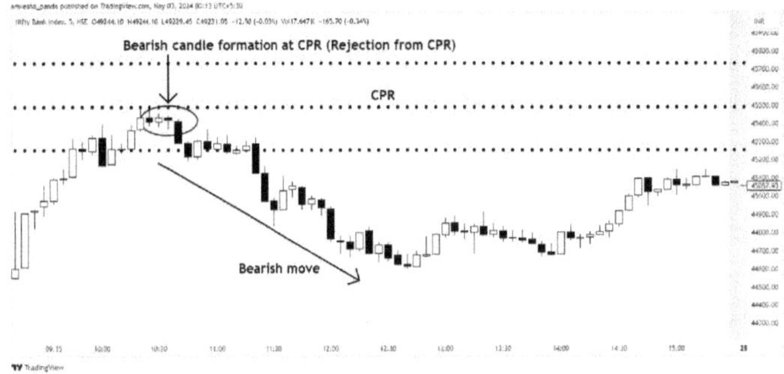

Figure (12.7)

Figure (12.8) showcases a 5-minute chart of the Nifty Bank Index on April 29, 2024, demonstrating the significant role of the Central Pivot Range (CPR) as a robust support level. The chart illustrates how the CPR acted as a strong support zone when the candles approached it. Upon reaching the CPR, the candles found support, initiating an upward momentum in price action that led to a bullish rally.

In such scenarios, traders can strategically capitalize on these movements by establishing long positions when they observe candles finding support at the CPR level. To manage risk effectively, traders can set stop-loss orders below the CPR level. This approach helps protect against adverse price movements while allowing traders to capture potential gains.

A prudent risk-reward strategy can further enhance trading outcomes. Traders may set a target for profit-taking at a ratio of 1:2 risk-reward, ensuring that potential gains outweigh potential losses. By combining technical analysis with effective risk management techniques, traders can optimize their trading strategies and capitalize on favorable market movements influenced by key support and resistance levels such as the CPR.

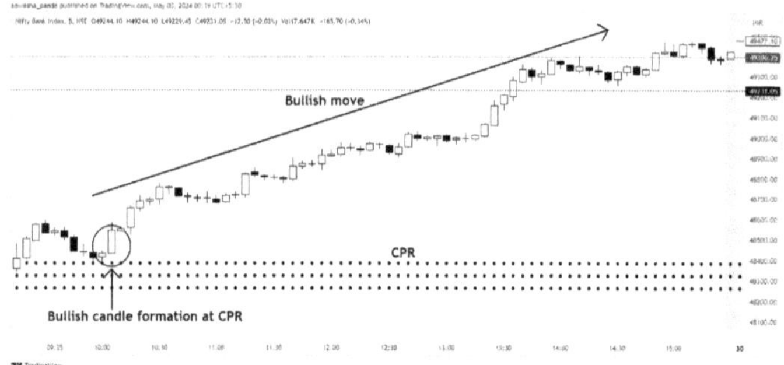

Figure (12.8)

Figure (12.9) illustrates the 5-minute chart of the Nifty 50 Index on March 15, 2024. It demonstrates that immediately after the market opened, a bearish candlestick pattern formed at the Central Pivot Range (CPR). This pattern caused the price to encounter resistance, resulting in bearish momentum in price action and triggering a downward rally.

Traders can take advantage of this market movement by entering short trades after confirming the bearish candle pattern at the CPR. It's important to be mindful that the price may face resistance at the CPR level, potentially leading to a downward rally. To manage risk effectively, traders can place stop-loss orders either above the CPR level or based on a 1:2 risk-reward ratio, adjusting according to their risk tolerance and trading strategy.

Figure (12.9)

Figure (12.10) displays the 5-minute chart of the Nifty 50 Index on February 19, 2024. It illustrates how, following a brief period of downward momentum, the candles found support at the Central Pivot Range (CPR). Subsequently, bullish candlestick patterns formed on the CPR, further confirming the support, and initiating a bullish rally.

Traders can capitalize on this favorable setup by initiating long positions upon confirmation of candles finding support at the CPR level. To manage risk effectively, traders may place stop-loss orders either below the CPR level or based on a risk-reward ratio of 1:2, aligning with their risk tolerance and trading strategy. This approach allows traders to participate in and potentially profit from the ensuing bullish move in price action.

Figure (12.10)

• • •

CHAPTER XIII

DAY HIGH/ DAY LOW BREAKOUT STRATEGY

Previous day high (PDH) and previous day low (PDL) are crucial levels that should be marked on the chart as they serve as strong support and resistance levels for day trading. These levels remain effective in all market conditions, whether the market is trending or sideways. However, on a trending day, if the market breaks above the previous day high or below the previous day low with a strong candle, there is a high probability that the market will continue to trend further in the same direction beyond these levels. Therefore, traders often monitor these levels closely and consider them in their trading strategies to identify potential breakout opportunities and gauge the strength of the prevailing trend.

Before entering any trades based on breaks of previous day high (PDH) or previous day low (PDL), it's crucial to consider an important factor. Ensure that there are no significant support or resistance levels nearby, either just above PDH or just below PDL. If such levels exist in close proximity, it limits the space for price movement and increases the likelihood of a potential reversal. This precautionary step helps traders avoid getting caught in false breakouts and ensures they enter trades with adequate room for price continuation in the intended direction. Incorporating this consideration into your trading strategy enhances the probability of successful trades and reduces the risk of unexpected market reversals.

The 5-minute chart of the Nifty 50 Index on November 15, 2023 and November 16, 2023, showcased in Figure (13.1), presents an insightful scenario that traders often encounter in technical analysis and trading strategies. November 15, 2023, marked a day of range-bound/ sideways trading, characterized by price movements confined within a specific range without a clear directional bias. Traders and analysts closely monitor such sessions as they indicate potential market indecision and accumulation of trading positions.

The significance of range-bound days lies in their role as precursors to potential breakout or breakdown events in the market. Traders who anticipate and prepare for such scenarios can position themselves advantageously to capitalize on subsequent trending movements. In the case of Figure (13.1), the range-bound day on November 15, 2023, set the stage for a potential breakout opportunity on November 16, 2023.

On November 16, 2023, the chart shows a bullish candle breaking above the previous day's high, marking a decisive breakout from the range-bound market conditions of the previous day. This breakout not only breached a key resistance level represented by the previous day's high but also triggered a notable upward momentum in price action. Market participants reacting to this breakout likely entered long positions, contributing to a significant rally in the market.

This example underscores the importance of monitoring range-bound days and identifying breakout patterns for trading strategies. Breakout strategies often involve entering positions after confirming a breakout from key levels, such as previous day highs or lows. Traders who use technical analysis tools in conjunction with price action observations can gain valuable insights into market dynamics and potential trading opportunities.

Figure (13.1)

Figure (13.2) showcases the 5-minute chart of the Nifty 50 Index on October 20, 2023 and October 23, 2023, highlighting an interesting aspect of technical analysis and trading strategies. October 20, 2023, unfolded as a day marked by range-bound/sideways trading, where the price movement remained confined within a specific range without a clear directional bias. Traders often monitor such days closely as they may indicate potential shifts in market sentiment or upcoming breakout opportunities.

The significance of range-bound days lies in their potential to precede breakout or breakdown events in the market. Traders who recognize these patterns and act decisively can position themselves strategically for potential trending movements. In the context of Figure (13.2), the range-bound conditions on October 20, 2023, set the stage for a potential breakout scenario on October 23, 2023.

On October 20, 2023, the chart displays a bearish candle breaking below the previous day's low, signaling a decisive breakout from the range-bound market conditions of the previous day. This breakout not only breached a key support level represented by the previous day's low but also triggered a notable downward momentum in price action. Traders leveraging breakout strategies likely entered short positions or adjusted their strategies to capitalize on the downward movement.

The example from Figure (13.2) highlights the importance of recognizing breakout patterns and using technical analysis to confirm such market shifts. Breakouts from key levels, such as previous day lows or highs, often indicate shifts in market sentiment and the potential for sustained directional movements. Traders combining technical analysis tools with price action observations can gain valuable insights into market dynamics and make informed trading decisions.

Figure (13.2)

Figure (13.3) depicts the 5-minute chart of the Nifty Bank Index on October 20, 2023 and October 23, 2023, respectively. It is evident that October 20, 2023, was characterized by a complete range-bound/sideways trading session. Therefore, one might anticipate that the following day, October 23, 2023, would exhibit a trending market.

As observed in figure (13.3), on October 20, 2023, a bearish candle broke below the previous day's low. This breakout signaled a downward momentum in price action, leading to a significant downward rally in the market.

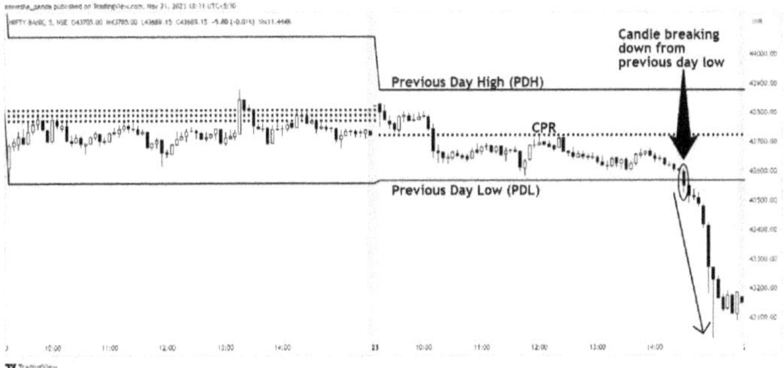

Figure (13.3)

Figure (13.4) depicts the 5-minute chart of the Nifty Bank Index on October 9, 2023 and October 10, 2023. It is evident that October 9, 2023, was characterized by a complete range-bound trading session. Therefore, one might anticipate that the following day, October 10, 2023, would exhibit a trending market.

As observed in figure (13.4), on October 10, 2023, a bullish candle broke above the previous day's high. This breakout signaled an upward momentum in price action, leading to a significant upward rally in the market.

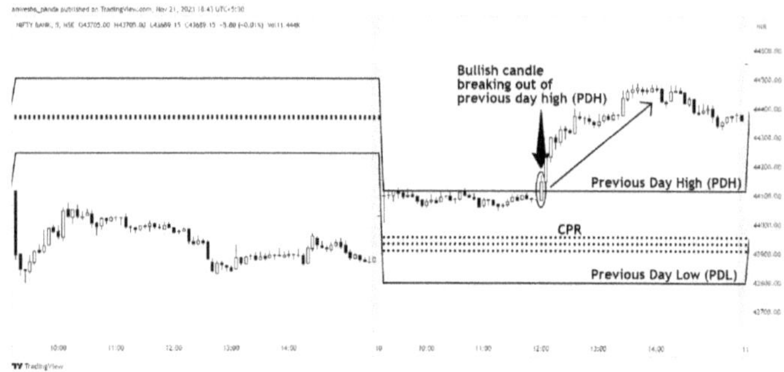

Figure (13.4)

In the context of Figure (13.5), which showcases the 5-minute chart of the Nifty Bank Index on February 29, 2024 and March 1, 2024, we delve into the dynamics of range-bound markets and subsequent trending movements. February 29, 2024, marked a day of consolidation, where the market lacked a clear directional bias and traded within a defined range. Such days are crucial for traders as they set the stage for potential breakout or breakdown scenarios. Traders often anticipate that after a range-bound day, the subsequent trading session may exhibit a trending market, driven by a decisive move breaking the consolidation range.

On March 1, 2024, the chart reveals a notable event—the first 5-minute candle of the day appeared as a large bullish candle, signaling a bullish breakout above the previous day's high. This breakout not only breached a key resistance level but also triggered an upward momentum in price action. The bullish sentiment was further reinforced as the market participants reacted positively to the breakout, leading to a significant rally in the market.

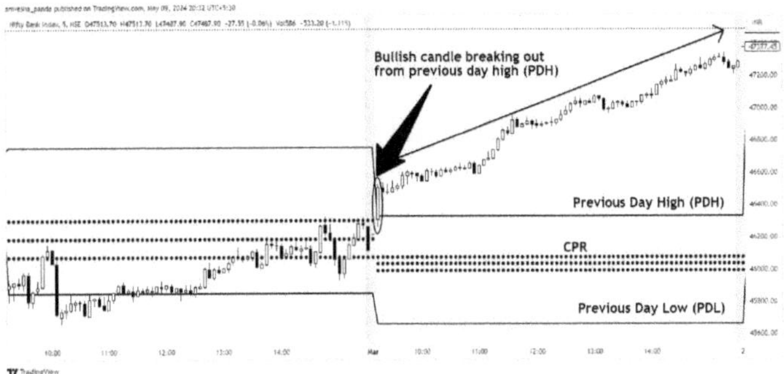

Figure (13.5)

This scenario exemplifies the importance of understanding market structures, such as range-bound days and breakout patterns, in trading analysis. Traders who identify such patterns and anticipate potential breakouts or breakdowns can position themselves strategically to capitalize on emerging trends. Breakout trading strategies often involve entering positions after confirming a breakout from key levels, in this case, the previous day's high. It highlights the proactive approach required in trading, where traders monitor price movements, key levels, and market sentiment to execute well-informed and timely trades.

Moreover, this example underscores the significance of technical analysis tools and price action observations in guiding trading decisions. By combining technical analysis with an understanding of market psychology and momentum, traders can gain insights into potential market directions and identify profitable trading opportunities.

• • •

CHAPTER XIV

RISK MANAGEMENT & POSITION SIZING

Trading involves identifying and following the direction of the dominant market trend. However, it comes with its own challenges and risks, such as false signals, whipsaws, drawdowns, and changing market regimes. Therefore, it is essential to incorporate risk management and position sizing in your trading strategies to ensure that your strategy is robust, consistent, and profitable in the long run.

As a trader, your first duty is to protect your capital. Your capital is the source to making money in the market. The most common reason why people lose money in the market is greed. They participate in the market and take positions as if there is no tommorow. They forget the fact that market is here to stay. Little do they know that the market is supreme and it will hardly take a few seconds for the market to wipe out there entire capital, if they take rash decisions in greed. Many new traders make the mistake of taking on large positions, in the belief that they will make easy and quick profits. In the long run, this type of behaviour more often ends in despair over large losses than the opposite. This is where risk management and position sizing come into play.

Risk management and position sizing are very crucial aspects of successful trading and aim to protect traders from significant losses and preserve capital. The primary goal of risk management is to strike a balance between maximizing profits and minimizing the potential for adverse outcomes.

RISK MANAGEMENT

Risk management in trading involves several principles and strategies aimed at minimizing potential losses. While there isn't a single formula for risk management in trading, there are various techniques traders use to manage risk effectively. Here are some key components and strategies.

1. **Position Sizing:** Determining the size of each trade based on the level of risk you're willing to take on a single trade. Techniques like the Fixed Fractional, Fixed Ratio, or Percentage of Portfolio methods help control the amount of capital risked per trade.
2. **Stop Loss Orders:** Setting predetermined points at which you will exit a trade to limit losses. This order helps to automatically sell a security when it reaches a certain price, preventing further losses beyond a set threshold.
3. **Risk-Reward Ratio:** Assessing the potential profit against the potential loss before entering a trade. A common practice is aiming for a higher potential reward compared to the potential risk, like a 2:1 or 3:1 ratio.
4. **Diversification:** Spreading investments across different asset classes or securities to reduce overall risk. This includes diversification by industry, geography, or asset type.
5. **Risk Assessment:** Evaluating the overall risk exposure of your portfolio. This involves understanding correlations between different assets and considering how they might behave in various market conditions.

6. **Adaptability and Flexibility:** Being adaptable to market changes and willing to adjust strategies based on market conditions, news events, or shifts in volatility.

There isn't a single formula that fits all trading situations due to the dynamic nature of markets and individual trading styles. Risk management often involves a combination of these techniques tailored to the trader's risk tolerance, investment horizon, and overall trading strategy. Traders often backtest different risk management approaches to see what fits their style and helps them achieve their financial goals while managing risk effectively.

POSITION SIZING

Position sizing in trading refers to determining the amount of capital to allocate to a particular trade. The goal is to manage risk by controlling the amount of money invested in any single trade. Here is a common formula used for position sizing.

Position Size = (Account Size × Risk Amount)/Stop Loss Distance

FIXED FRACTIONAL POSITION SIZING

Fixed fractional position sizing is a risk management strategy used by traders to determine the size of their positions in each trade based on a fixed percentage of their total trading capital.

- **Percentage Risk:** Traders decide on a fixed percentage of their trading capital to risk per trade. This percentage is often referred to as the risk per trade or risk percentage. For example, a trader may decide to risk 2% of their total trading capital on each trade.

- **Position Size Calculation:** Once the risk percentage is determined, traders calculate the position size for each trade based on this percentage and the size of their trading capital. For example, if a trader's total trading capital is Rs 10,000 and they decide to risk 2% per trade, their position size would be: *Position Size = (2 / 100) * 10,000 = 200.*
- **Risk Management:** By using fixed fractional position sizing, traders ensure that the amount of capital risked per trade adjusts dynamically based on the size of their trading account. This helps protect their capital during periods of drawdown and allows for consistent risk management across different trades.

These formulas aim to help traders control risk by standardizing the amount of capital allocated to each trade based on their risk tolerance, account size, and specific trade parameters like stop loss distance or volatility. Traders often choose the position sizing method that aligns best with their trading strategy and risk management preferences.

IMPORTANCE OF RISK MANAGEMENT & POSITION SIZING IN TRADING

Risk management and position sizing is crucial in trading and investing for several reasons:

1. **Limit Risk:** It helps to control and manage the amount of money put at risk in any single trade. By setting a

maximum loss amount per trade, you can protect your capital from significant depletion caused due to a single unfavorable trade.

2. **Preservation of Capital:** Proper position sizing safeguards against large losses that could potentially wipe out a substantial portion of your capital. By limiting the amount risked per trade, you can sustain losses without devastating overall portfolio.

3. **Consistency in Risk:** Position sizing maintains a consistent level of risk across trades. Whether you are dealing with high or low volatility stocks, it ensures that each trade carries a proportionate risk level based on pre-determined criteria (e.g. percentage of total capital).

4. **Emotional Control:** Properly sizing positions can help mitigate emotional responses to trading. When a trade is appropriately sized, the potential loss is predefined, reducing the likelihood of impulsive decisions based on fear or greed.

5. **Adaptability and Flexibility:** Position sizing allows to adapt strategies to different market conditions. During volatile periods, for instance, smaller position sizes might be employed to account for increased risk.

6. **Improvement and Consistency in Trading Performance:** Consistent and effective position sizing can improve overall trading performance. By focusing on risk management, you can protect your capital and stay in the game long enough to benefit from profitable trades.

7. **Long-Term Sustainability:** Controlling position sizes is crucial for long-term sustainability in trading. Even with a series of losing trades, proper risk management through position sizing ensures that the impact on the

overall trading capital is manageable, allowing you to recover more easily.

Risk management and position sizing play crucial roles not only in protecting against losses but also in fostering consistency and discipline in trading practices. These strategies are essential pillars that help traders navigate market uncertainties, adapt to changing conditions, and maintain a focused approach towards long-term profitability. A robust risk management framework combined with appropriate position sizing is integral to achieving sustainable success in trading and effectively managing the complexities of financial markets.

Position sizing, a fundamental aspect of risk management in trading, ensures that traders remain within their predefined risk tolerance levels while safeguarding their capital. It promotes a disciplined approach to trading, especially in volatile and uncertain market environments. By carefully determining the size of each position based on risk parameters, traders can mitigate potential losses and optimize returns over time. This disciplined approach not only protects against excessive risk-taking but also instills confidence and consistency in trading decisions.

Successful traders understand that proper risk management and position sizing are not optional but essential practices for longevity in trading. They enable traders to survive and thrive in diverse market conditions, preventing catastrophic losses and preserving capital for profitable opportunities. Emphasizing risk management and disciplined position sizing ultimately contributes to sustainable and successful trading journeys in the dynamic realm of financial markets.

• • •

CHAPTER XV

TRADING PSYCHOLOGY

Trading psychology refers to the mental and emotional factors that influence a trader's behavior, decisions, and overall mindset while participating in financial markets. It encompasses various psychological elements that impact trading activities, including emotions like fear, greed, hope, and anxiety, which can significantly influence trading decisions. Fear of losses might prompt premature exits from profitable trades, while greed could lead to taking excessive risks, ultimately resulting in the loss of the entire capital.

Controlling emotions is crucial for making rational and disciplined trading decisions, which can ensure a trader's profitability in the long term. A trader's mindset and discipline play a significant role in their success. Having a clear trading plan, following predefined strategies, and maintaining discipline in adhering to rules are essential components of a successful trader's mindset.

Proper risk management is not just about formulas and calculations; it also involves the psychological aspect of accepting and managing risk. Traders need to balance risk and reward and avoid taking excessive risks due to overconfidence or fear. Successful trading requires patience. Traders often face the temptation to overtrade or deviate from their strategy due to impulsive decisions. Developing the ability to wait for the right opportunities and exercise restraint is crucial.

Markets are dynamic, and traders need to adapt to changing conditions. Being flexible and able to adjust strategies without emotional bias is a vital aspect of trading psychology. Traders often face losses or setbacks. Having a resilient mindset that allows one to learn from mistakes, rather than being discouraged or making emotional decisions, is crucial for improvement.

Cognitive biases such as confirmation bias, recency bias, or anchoring can influence decision-making. Recognizing and mitigating these biases is essential for making objective trading decisions.

CULTIVATING A STRONG TRADING PSYCHOLOGY FOR PEAK PERFORMANCE

Developing a strong trading psychology is an ongoing process that involves self-awareness, discipline, and consistent effort. Here are steps to help cultivate a proper trading psychology.

1. **Self-Awareness:** Understand your emotions, biases, and triggers that affect your trading decisions. Keep a trading journal to track your thoughts, emotions, and actions during trades. This helps identify patterns and areas for improvement.
2. **Establish a Trading Plan:** Create a well-defined trading plan with clear entry and exit criteria, risk management rules, and guidelines for various market scenarios. Having a plan reduces uncertainty and emotional reactions.
3. **Risk Management:** Prioritize risk management. Define your risk tolerance and set stop loss levels for each trade based on your risk-reward ratio. Stick to these levels to control losses and minimize emotional influence.

4. **Practice Discipline:** Follow your trading plan rigorously. Discipline is crucial in avoiding impulsive decisions driven by emotions. Avoid deviating from your strategy due to fear, greed, or FOMO (Fear of Missing Out).

5. **Manage Expectations:** Realize that losses are a part of trading. Focus on consistency and managing risk rather than expecting every trade to be profitable. Set realistic goals and avoid chasing unrealistic returns.

6. **Continuous Learning:** Constantly seek to improve your knowledge and skills. Stay updated on market developments and trading strategies.

7. **Control Emotions:** Develop techniques to manage emotions. Techniques like meditation, deep breathing, or taking breaks during stressful periods can help maintain emotional balance.

8. **Backtesting and Analysis:** Backtest your strategies to gain confidence in their effectiveness. Analyze past trades to understand what worked and what didn't, learning from both successes and failures.

9. **Mindfulness and Mental Health:** Take care of your mental and physical well-being. Practice mindfulness, exercise, and maintain a healthy lifestyle to reduce stress and improve decision-making.

10. **Patience and Persistence:** Cultivate patience and persistence. Trading psychology takes time to develop. Be patient with yourself and persistently work on improving your mindset and approach.

Developing a proper trading psychology is an ongoing journey that involves both technical and psychological aspects. It's about managing emotions, maintaining discipline, and continuously refining your approach to become a more effective and successful trader.

Trading psychology encompasses more than just knowledge of markets or technical analysis; it involves understanding oneself as a trader and cultivating the mental discipline and emotional control necessary to navigate the uncertainties and challenges of trading. Successful traders often emphasize the pivotal role of psychological factors in achieving overall trading success. It is fundamental to recognize that trading psychology is a cornerstone of successful trading endeavors.

Effective trading is not solely about analyzing charts and making predictions; it's equally about managing emotions, maintaining discipline, and making rational decisions amidst market volatility and unpredictability. Traders who prioritize developing a robust psychological foundation often find it easier to navigate the complexities of financial markets and emerge as successful traders and investors.

By acknowledging and addressing psychological aspects such as fear, greed, patience, and resilience, traders can enhance their decision-making processes and improve overall trading outcomes. Building emotional intelligence and mental fortitude enables traders to stay focused during challenging market conditions, avoid impulsive actions, and stick to well-defined trading strategies.

Moreover, trading psychology extends beyond individual trades; it influences long-term trading performance and sustainability. Cultivating a positive mindset, learning from mistakes, and adapting to changing market dynamics are integral parts of a trader's psychological journey. Embracing a growth mindset allows traders to view setbacks as learning opportunities and continuously improve their skills and strategies.

In essence, while technical analysis and market knowledge are essential components of trading success, mastering trading psychology is equally crucial. It empowers traders to make informed decisions based on logic and analysis rather than emotions and impulses, contributing significantly to long-term trading success and profitability.

• • •

www.ingramcontent.com/pod-product-compliance
Lightning Source LLC
Chambersburg PA
CBHW040738120726

48007CB00008B/127